What Every Great Salesperson Knows

A No Nonsense Guide For Sales Success
Practical Self Assessments, Effective Exercises and Actual Case Studies

Robert Arzt, CLU, ChFC, LLIF
and
Howard Russell, Ph.D.

Champions Publishing Co.
Rockville, MD

Library of Congress Cataloguing-in-Publication Data
Arzt, Robert 2009
What every great salesperson knows: a no-nonsense guide for sales success /
Robert Arzt
ISBN (cloth): 978-0-615-30380-2
1. Insurance—Sales Training.   2. Sales—Personal Development   I. Arzt, Robert.
II. Title.

Published in the United States by

Champions Publishing Co.
10216 Sweetwood Ave.
Rockville, MD 20850

First Edition

Contents

Preface

I am passionate about the financial services industry. To be more specific, I am passionate about the sales professionals within the industry and the tremendous amount of good that they do for individuals, businesses, and families.

My dad, who suffered from cancer for over twenty years, died when I was eighteen. He sold insurance during the last two years of his life and subsequently came to have a keen appreciation for how much good it can do. He once commented to me that if he had the opportunity to plan his professional life all over again, he would start his career in the insurance business. I took his words to heart and began my career in insurance at the age of twenty-seven. At that time, I had already graduated from college, been married for almost 6 and 1/2 years, and just learned that our first child was on the way.

The financial services industry and being an entrepreneur living on 100% commissions gave me the opportunity to grow personally and professionally. I was on a quest to learn what made a great salesperson. I wanted to know what steps I could take to emulate the success principles of highly successful salespeople. I was surrounded by excellent, positive associates and exposed to all of the inspirational classics, such as *Think and Grow Rich* by Napoleon Hill, *The Power of Positive Thinking* by Norman Vincent Peale, *The Magic of Believing* by Claude Bristol, *The Strangest Secret* by Earl Nightingale and *A Success System that Never Fails* by W. Clement Stone. I entered the industry at the time that audio cassette tape programs were in vogue, and I took full advantage of them by listening for scores of hours.

Later in my career, I switched roles from salesperson to sales supervisor to home office employee to home office executive in charge of the training and development of sales producers and sales managers. During this time, I came to realize that everyone is looking for someone to help them be or become all that they are capable of.

I also observed that many who enter the sales profession have the misfortune of working with less than capable managers and supervisors. Therefore, in my role as VP of training, I sought to create programs that taught salespeople how to be successful—whether their managers were up to the task or not.

I eventually left the corporate financial services world for a career in an educational non-profit that provided sales and product training to the financial services industry. By doing so, I extended my reach manyfold.

I founded Polaris One and Insurance Coach U™ to help salespeople and sales managers be the best they could be by teaching them how to provide their clients with the best they have to offer. This book is a synthesis of what I've learned. I hope you will find the information, exercises and tools presented here both useful and inspirational. You are a member of a unique and valuable profession that will bring you many rewards—not only financially, but also professionally and personally.

May you have a wonderful journey!
Bob Arzt, CLU, ChFC, LLIF

Acknowledgments

I am truly grateful to the many people who have had a positive influence on my life and who have inspired me to pursue the career for which I was destined. It is impossible to thank each one individually, but I would like to acknowledge a few by name.

I thank my parents (now both deceased) for their unconditional love and support. Both of them taught me courage and perseverance in the face of adversity. Glenn B. Dorr Jr. gave me the opportunity to join the financial services industry. Through his example, Art Gershenbaum, a sales associate, kept me going when times were tough. Ron Willingham, a truly gifted entrepreneur has always been an inspiration to me. Clarice Dankers, a talented editor, used her insights to help me move this book from draft to mission accomplished.

I would also like to thank Howard Russell, Ph.D., for his friendship over the last 25 years and for his collaboration on this book. And I thank my coaching clients, who have taken that extra step forward to grow and evolve to their next level, for their trust, faith, and confidence.

These acknowledgements would not be complete without mentioning Jennifer and Megan, my daughters. I am so proud of their accomplishments and inspired by their vigor for pursuing lives of fullness and fulfillment!

Above all, I would like to acknowledge my wife Terry, who has been with me since the beginning. We met in 1968 and have been together ever since. Terry has influenced and inspired me. She possesses that rare quality of making everyone in her life feel special. Her love, encouragement, unconditional support, and guidance (both when asked for and not) have helped me with my journey.

 # Introduction

The Theory Behind This Book

What Every Great Salesperson Knows is a personal development workbook for sales professionals who want to achieve success in sales. If you are new to sales, it will help you get your career off to a flying start. If you are an experienced professional, it will help you achieve new levels of success. It will also help you find meaning, fulfillment and exhilaration in your sales career.

In contrast to other books on sales, this workbook does not focus simply on knowing your company's products and services or even on knowledge of the steps in the sales cycle. Instead, it focuses on the personal qualities necessary to achieve excellence in sales.

This book is based on extensive research regarding what it takes to achieve success in a sales career; in particular, it focuses on the Six Critical Prerequisites and the 15 Sales Success Factors.

The Six Critical Prerequisites

Findings indicate that there are six critical prerequisites to achieving success in sales:

1. **An unwavering commitment** to a sales career mission that is in line with your personal values.

2. **A vision** that provides a detailed mental picture of the future you want to create for your sales career as you pursue your mission.

3. **Clearly-defined goals** in which you specify what you need to achieve to make your vision a reality.

4. **Mastery of the sales success factors,** or the behaviors, motives, attitudes, traits, and self-concepts that contribute to superior sales performance.

5. **Action plans** that provide road maps for accessing people and resources and for using the sales success factors to achieve your goals.

6. **A way to maintain progress** on the journey until your vision of success becomes reality.

Each of these prerequisites is addressed throughout this book, along with ample opportunities to practice each one.

The 15 Sales Success Factors

The heart of this book focuses on the 15 distinct **sales competencies, or success factors**, shown to be of particular importance for intermediate- to long-cycle selling. Such cycles require positive interpersonal interactions to clarify and respond to customer needs, generate sales, retain customers, and develop repeat business.

The data on sales competencies was compiled over a 20-year period by researchers looking to discover the measurable personal characteristics that make the difference between top performers and average performers in a specific job. The findings from these studies have been combined and updated for this book.

As illustrated in the table below, each of the competencies has been assigned to the four basic categories of management.

The 15 Sales Success Factors	

Mastery of Self
  1. Shows self-discipline
  2. Has self-confidence
  3. Maintains self-control
  4. Assesses self accurately
	Mastery of Customer Relationships
	  9. Focuses on customer success
	  10. Has interpersonal sensitivity
	  11. Gains commitment

Mastery of the Sales Process
  5. Has a results orientation
  6. Is Adaptable
  7. Questions & listens effectively
  8. Applies targeted problem solving
	Mastery of Own Business
	  12. Has entrepreneurial drive
	  13. Uses key information effectively
	  14. Increases customer value
	  15. Builds a team

Why This Book Is Different

> To discover = *To gain knowledge through observation, study, or search*
> —Merriam-Webster's Collegiate Dictionary, Eleventh Edition

This book takes a different approach from the usual treatises on sales in that it doesn't simply describe the competency models of sales success, but shows you how to work with and apply them in your own life and career. It also provides numerous exercises that give you the opportunity to compare *your* strengths with those of top-performing sales professionals and teaches you why, when and how to apply the models to achieve your own outstanding results.

That's where *to discover* comes in. Because it is a verb, *to discover* implies taking action. Although simply reading the information presented here will doubtless help you improve your sales success, actively participating in the learning and discovery process will skyrocket it.

The results you can expect when you put this program into practice will be phenomenal. Over time, you will change the way you think about yourself and the future of your career. Your knowledge of what is possible—professionally and personally—will expand exponentially, and your business will follow suit.

A Word About Adult Learning Theory

> *I hear and I forget, I see and I remember, I do and I understand.*
> —Confucius

To make it as easy as possible for you to internalize and practice the concepts presented here, the information has been designed according to the latest theories of adult learning. For example:

Adults learn best when they become conscious of a need and recognize that it is their responsibility to find a solution for it. The solution, whether it be a book, seminar, lecture, or training event, must be relevant to an individual's self-perceived need. This is why it is important to ask yourself: "What expectations and outcomes do I have for myself concerning the needs I have identified? What commitments am I willing to make to achieve the results I desire?

Adults learn best when they receive clear, honest, detailed feedback from others. Praise, recognition, encouragement and approval are some of the best catalysts for sparking the motivation to improve. These can come from a coworker, spouse, manager, significant other, mentor, or personal coach. Therefore, the book gives you numerous opportunities to rate yourself in a given area and to obtain feedback from those you trust and respect.

Adults learn best when the material pertains to their real lives and when they actively participate in the learning process. Therefore, the exercises focus on your particular challenges. For example, the book asks you to develop your own vision and mission statements, critique yourself, and receive feedback about your strengths in each competency. It also asks you numerous questions to check your knowledge and understanding of the topics and concepts it presents.

Adults learn from real-life stories about people who have achieved success using similar tools and techniques. Therefore, the book includes inspiring case studies of real people who have successfully applied these principles and achieved superior results.

Adults learn best using a "do it, learn from it, analyze it, and do it again" action model. Knowledge for knowledge's sake is nice, but knowledge turned into effective action and applied to real-life situations produces results. Therefore, each chapter offers numerous examples, case studies and exercises.

Chapter Overview

The rest of this book is organized as follows.

Chapter 2: Vision and Mission Statements

A critical element in the accomplishment of any goal is knowing what you want to achieve and what your motivations are for achieving it. Chapter 2 takes you step-by-step through this process; by the time you have completed all of the exercises, you will have a clear understanding of where you want to go with your sales career and why you want to go there.

Chapter 3: The Personal Psychology of Sales Success

Chapter 3 explores the various personal psychological elements necessary for success in sales. These include a willingness to participate in the continual performance improvement process and an understanding of how flow, attention and focus influence motivation, commitment and values.

Chapter 4: Sales Success Factor Questionnaire

Chapter 4 consists of the Sales Success Factor Questionnaire. The questionnaire gives you the opportunity to evaluate yourself and rate how you use the 15 core success factors of people who excel at sales. The results will clearly demonstrate for you the success factors that are your strengths and the ones you need to focus on for further development.

Chapters 5 through 8: The 15 Sales Success Factors

Chapters 5 through 8 take you through each Sales Success Factor in depth. They also provide numerous exercises to help you understand, explore and apply each factor successfully.

Chapter 9: Conclusion

Chapter 9 brings all of what you have learned together and suggests where to go from here.

Chapter 2   Your Sales Career Vision and Mission

One of the most important steps you can take in your sales career is to develop and write down vision and mission statements that clearly define what you want to accomplish in your sales career and why you want to accomplish it. Because they play such a critical role in your ability to succeed, the book begins with them.

The Power of a Personal Vision

One of my coaching clients, Jeff, was an excellent life insurance salesperson—that is, when he was actually talking to a client. Otherwise, he didn't accomplish much. He told me that his problem was a lack of organization, and it certainly looked that way on the surface. After coaching him for just one hour, however, it became clear to me that Jeff's fundamental problem was the absence of an overall vision for his practice. In fact, his only conscious goal was to earn enough money to pay his bills.

Because Jeff did not know what he ultimately wished to achieve—or why—he was unable to stay on track with his business. Each day buffeted him from one crisis to another like a butterfly trying to fly into the wind. That is why I advised him to create a clear vision statement for his practice using the steps described in this chapter.

Once Jeff knew where he was going and why, he created specific action plans with measurable steps and timeframes for each of his long-term and short-term goals. Today he approaches each day deliberately, with a clear focus. He has increased his schedule of weekly appointments by 50%, has more energy, is optimistic about the future, and takes pride in the benefits and services he provides his prospects and clients. Thanks to his clear vision, he is now positioned to expand his practice well into the future.

Your Sales Career Vision Statement

Now it's your turn.

Formulating your sales career vision begins with the need to make some choices. At this point, you may not be fully aware of all the stimulating and satisfying options ahead of you in your sales career. That's all right. You can expand your vision as your experience grows.

Step I: Visualize A Picture Of Your Future Sales Career

The first step is to find a quiet place where you can be by yourself for at least 30 minutes. You are going to visualize a time in the future—perhaps two or three years—and observe what is happening in each area of your life (as depicted below). As you do, jot down a few notes about what you see. Note: be sure to write in the present tense (I am earning/I earn) *as though it were true for you right now.*
To begin, follow these steps:

1. In the form on the next page, write down the future date you wish to use for this exercise.

2. Close your eyes and take a few deep breaths. Tense your entire body and hold for a few seconds. Then release the tension and take a few more deep breaths.

3. Read question 1-A (your level of compensation), then close your eyes. Allow your mind to bring you a sum that you would like to be earning by the date you have selected. Write this figure down on the form in the present tense. (I am easily earning ___ every month.)

4. Next, read question 1-B (career advancements you are enjoying). Using all of your senses (sight, smell, taste, sound, touch), imagine how much you are enjoying your advancement. What is the expression on your face? How do you feel? Where are you? Who are you with? Write down what you "see" using the present tense.

5. Continue this process until you have filled in all of the sections of the form.

My Sales Career

The target date for my vision is: _______/_______/_______

I. My Achievements

    A. My level of compensation

    B. Career advancements I am enjoying

    C. Recognition I have received for my sales success

II. My Relationships
A. People on my team
B. Types of relationships I have with my peers
C. Profile of my best customers
D. The way my customers feel about me
E. How I feel about my customers
F. My family relationships

<table>
<tr><td colspan="1">III. My Impact</td></tr>
<tr><td>A. My reputation</td></tr>
<tr><td>B. My leadership roles</td></tr>
<tr><td>C. Marketing, prospecting and sales strategies I have in place</td></tr>
<tr><td>D. The things I own that reflect my success</td></tr>
<tr><td>E. My work environment at the office</td></tr>
</table>

IV. How I Experience Freedom

A. How I use my time

B. Where I go

C. What I do

D. The things I own that reflect my success

E. My work environment at the office

V. What I Do For Fun

A. Fun at work

B. Fun at leisure

Step II: Describe The Vision Of Your Sales Career In Writing

Now describe the vision of your sales career in writing. As you do, focus on the results you are experiencing, NOT on the steps you took to achieve them.

<table>
<tr><td>My Sales Career Vision Statement</td></tr>
<tr><td>

</td></tr>
</table>

Step III: Make A Choice

Finally, ask yourself: "If I could have this sales career, would I take it?" *Then make a choice.*

Your Sales Career Mission Statement

Now that you have a well-defined vision statement, the next step is to create a mission statement. Your career mission statement expresses your professional goals and what you stand for. It clearly describes who you are and what you want to accomplish in your sales career. A mission statement will guide you through all of the major career decisions you make, so it is well worth the time and effort it takes to get it right.

To get started, read the following examples of mission statements from other successful sales people. If one of them resonates with you, feel free to use it!

Examples of Mission Statements

- My mission is to continually improve my effectiveness in finding and responding to opportunities that help my clients solve their business needs.
- My mission is to find challenge, enjoyment and profit by exceeding my customers' expectations in identifying their needs and helping them achieve their personal and business financial goals.
- By knowing the economics and internal organization of the types of businesses I serve, I provide my clients with outstanding service and help them establish a long-lasting business relationship with my company that saves them time and money.
- My mission is to increase my income by continually initiating and building long-term, mutually-profitable relationships between my company, my clients and me.
- As an agent of ...(company name), my mission is to find enjoyment and profit by helping my clients identify and surmount obstacles to their financial success.

Step I: Define Your Personal Values

The first step in developing your mission statement is to brainstorm the personal values you hold, both for yourself and your career. This is because your personal values form the core of your sales career mission.

Examples of Personal Value Statements

To illustrate what I mean by a value statement, read the following examples from other successful sales people:

- I am a person who lives with great integrity.
- I always do the right thing because it is the right think to do.
- I always design my proposals around the needs my clients have expressed to me.
- I am surrounded constantly by incredible opportunities to help my clients.
- As a true professional and lifelong learner, I continually seek to increase my knowledge.

Now it's your turn

To get started, take a notepad and a pen or pencil and go to a quiet place where you will be undisturbed for at least 30 minutes. Take a few deep breaths and tense/relax the muscles in your body to center yourself. To start the flow of ideas, ask yourself the following questions:

1. What are my highest priorities as a human being?
2. What do I believe is important for me to think, feel, and do?
3. What is so important to me that I would be willing to undergo risk and discomfort to achieve it?

Give yourself the time and space you need to playfully come up with some answers. As you do, jot down your ideas as quickly as you can without judging their quality, grammatical correctness, or organization. Just write whatever comes to your mind first.

Once you have plenty of material to work with, take a look at what you have written and choose the statements and ideas that resonate most strongly for you. Write them in the box below.

My Personal Values

Step II: Define Your Sales Career Values

The second step in developing your mission statement is to brainstorm your sales career values. Following the same process as before, breathe, tense and relax. To get the process flowing, ask yourself the following questions:
1. What are my highest priorities for my sales career?
2. Why am I in this career?
3. What do I want to achieve in my sales career?
4. How do I want to think and feel when I am pursuing my career?
5. What do I want to accomplish so much in my sales career that I would be willing to undergo risk and discomfort to achieve it?

As your ideas begin to flow, write them in your notebook as quickly as you can.

Step III: Rank Your Sales Career Values

Once you have plenty of material to work with, review the sales career values you have written down. As you do, focus on statements that describe the purpose or priority of your sales career, NOT on goals that state specifically what you will achieve at some time in the future. Choose the sales career values that are most important to you and write them down in the following box. After you have created your list, rank your values in order of importance to you.

My Sales Career Values	Priority

After you have completed the reviewing and prioritizing process, examine your top priority statements. These will form the basis of your mission statement.

Step IV: Write Your Mission Statement

The third and final step is to write your mission statement. In crafting it, make sure it is:
True to your values: Say what is important to you, not what you think sounds good to someone else.
Concise: Make the statement brief, concrete and to the point.
Well-written: Be sure to use clear, grammatically-correct English so others can quickly grasp your meaning.
Dynamic: Use action verbs because your mission statement describes actions you plan to take and movements you plan to initiate.
Flexible: Make your statement open-ended enough that it offers various ways in which you can accomplish your purpose.

Remember that the purpose of your mission statement is to communicate who you are and what you stand for; it is NOT a list of goals and objectives.

My Sales Career Mission

Step V: Take a Break

Once you have written your mission statement, set it aside for a day or two. Then go back and reread it. Does it still make sense to you? Energize you? Light a spark within you? If it doesn't seem to express the essence of your mission anymore, revise it. If you can't quite put your finger on the problem, start the brainstorming process over again.

This statement will guide you in the development of your sales career goals, action plans and management systems, so make sure it is "right" before going on to the next step.

Step VI: Share Your Mission Statement With Others

When you feel comfortable with your mission statement, test it by sharing it with people you trust and respect. Ask them to evaluate your statement and let you know how realistic and clear it is. Also ask them to suggest ways in which you could improve it.

Your mission statement is meant to be shared with anyone who is affected by it. Therefore, you may want to share it with your prospects and customers. Doing so will help them understand your motivations for the career you have chosen. When your customers know your mission and share your enthusiasm for it, they will be eager to support you and help you stay on track. They will also be eager to give you leads to other people and organizations who could use your company's products and would enjoy doing business with you.

Your vision and mission statements are your guiding principles. They will govern the manner in which you conduct yourself and how you handle your business throughout your career, so it is important to take the time to get them right.

The Personal Psychology of Sales Success

The State of Flow

The intellect has little to do on the road to discovery. There comes a leap in consciousness, call it intuition or what you will, the solution comes to you and you don't know how or why.
—Albert Einstein

Your business practice has two components to it.

One is knowledge of your business. This includes knowing your products thoroughly and having a clear understanding of how they will benefit your clients. It includes knowing how to conduct a needs analysis for your clients. And it includes perfecting your presentation, time management and practice management skills.

But there is an even more important part of your business that largely determines your success: what is going on inside of you.

Changing your attitude makes all the difference

To clarify what I mean, let me tell you about one of my clients. Tom had been a salesman for years. He was never a superstar, but he didn't want to be. He made a decent living, so he was content. But in 2008, things began to change. It was subtle at first. At the beginning of the year, he noticed his sales closing ratios were off a little and that he had failed to schedule his usual number of appointments. Then he noticed that his revenues were down by 10%. As the year went on, his appointments, closing ratios, and referrals all dropped markedly.

Tom took this turn of events hard. He became more and more discouraged, could feel the lethargy in his step when he went to a sales appointment, and eventually became seriously depressed. He finally decided to make an appointment with a coach and called me.

"It isn't my fault," he sighed. "Everyone is having a hard time right now because of the economy."
In response, I told him that he had to decide.

"Decide what?" he asked.

"That this bad business cycle is over," I replied. "That you're done. That whatever happened in the past and why it happened has nothing to do with what will happen in the future. You must decide today that your future is going to be different."

I watched Tom's eyes as the light suddenly dawned in them. In that moment, he made a pivotal decision: to change the way he viewed his business and his abilities. Tom put new energy into generating sales appointments, making sales calls, and marketing. As a result, he began to feel better about himself and the future.

Soon after his "aha" moment, Tom was walking down a hallway to a sales appointment when he suddenly noticed there was a spring in his step again. He knew he had put together a proposal that was good for his client and he was eager to present it.

He also noticed something else. He didn't feel tied to the results of his upcoming sales call as he would have felt in the past. He walked into the appointment anticipating the joy he would feel just spending time with his client—whatever the outcome might be. During their meeting, the time flew by. Although Tom was working hard, he exuded confidence, easily answered every question, and addressed every objection perfectly. He knew his presentation had hit a home run.

And he quickly made the sale.

Being in the state of flow

What Tom experienced is called flow. It is what athletes call being in the zone or being in the groove. Flow describes the sense of seemingly effortless movement that occurs when we are in an optimal state. While it lasts, our thought processes work smoothly, and one action seamlessly follows another. We become so involved in what we're doing that the activity becomes spontaneous, almost automatic; in other words, we stop being aware of ourselves as separate from the actions we are performing.
One reason for this is that the concentration inherent in the flow process provides order to our thinking. Although it appears to be effortless, the experience often requires strenuous physical exertion, or highly disciplined mental activity. Any lapse of concentration will erase it.

A common feature of the flow experience is a **sense of discovery**, or the excitement of finding out something new about ourselves, such as our ability to meet and excel at challenges. When we're in the flow, there is no opportunity to reflect on or analyze ourselves because we're immersed in the activity in the present moment. Once it has ended, we often find that our sense of self emerges much clearer and stronger than before. We also discover that we've changed because our lives have been enriched by new skills, new awareness, and new achievements.

Recognizing Flow

You'll know you are in the flow when:
> You are so absorbed by an activity that your focus is completely in the present and your mind is clear, concentrated and alert.
> You feel motivated, self-confident and skillful.
> You have a sense of well-being and control, so you are completely open to whatever is happening in the moment.

Enemies of Flow

In contrast to the confidence we feel when we're in a flow experience, our day-to-day lives are often characterized by doubts, questions, and a preoccupation with ourselves. Because we feel threatened, we repeatedly question the necessity or wisdom of our actions and criticize our reasons for carrying them out.

> *Why am I doing this?*
> *Should I be doing something else?*

Without flow, everything we do is an effort. We constantly have the feeling that we are pushing a boulder uphill, that achieving our goals takes an inordinate amount of time, energy and effort. To develop the ability to stay in the flow, it is important to avoid the following:

- Caring what other people think
- Being tied to the outcome
- Becoming so comfortable with the status quo that we stop learning, growing, and setting new goals
- Being surrounded by negativity

Creating Flow

Almost anything can produce the flow experience providing that you:

Choose to act. Decide to get your energy moving any way you can. Tom forced himself to keep making appointments and seeing new clients; after a while, the momentum began to build and this step got easier and easier.

Visualize the end result. It's not necessary to visualize how a particular meeting or presentation will go. Simply focus on the end result, such as what level of business you will have achieved by the end of the year and how confident and successful you feel as a result.

Have confidence in the outcome. Don't simply tell yourself that "it would be nice, but..." Make a decision and then confidently expect a positive outcome.

Enjoy the journey. Above all, enjoy the process. Focus on how great it feels to build relationships with your clients, knowing how much you can help them. Remind yourself why you got into the business to begin with, how much you enjoy it, and how fun it is to reach your goals.

Develop clarity. Write down your goals so that you clearly understand what they are, why you want to achieve them, and what you need to do to get there.

Make a decision. Set your intention. Tom didn't tell himself that it would be nice to get his business back on track but... He decided that he was going to get his closing ratios back to where they were. Period. This is a game changer.

Make a commitment to yourself. Commit yourself to excellence. If your skills aren't good enough to achieve the outcome you desire, develop them.

The Next Step

Now that you understand the psychology of the flow process—and have made a firm commitment to yourself to change your future starting today—the next step is to commit yourself to the process of continual performance improvement.

The Continual Performance Improvement Process

Adopting the following model as a guide guarantees you on-going success in achieving your goals.

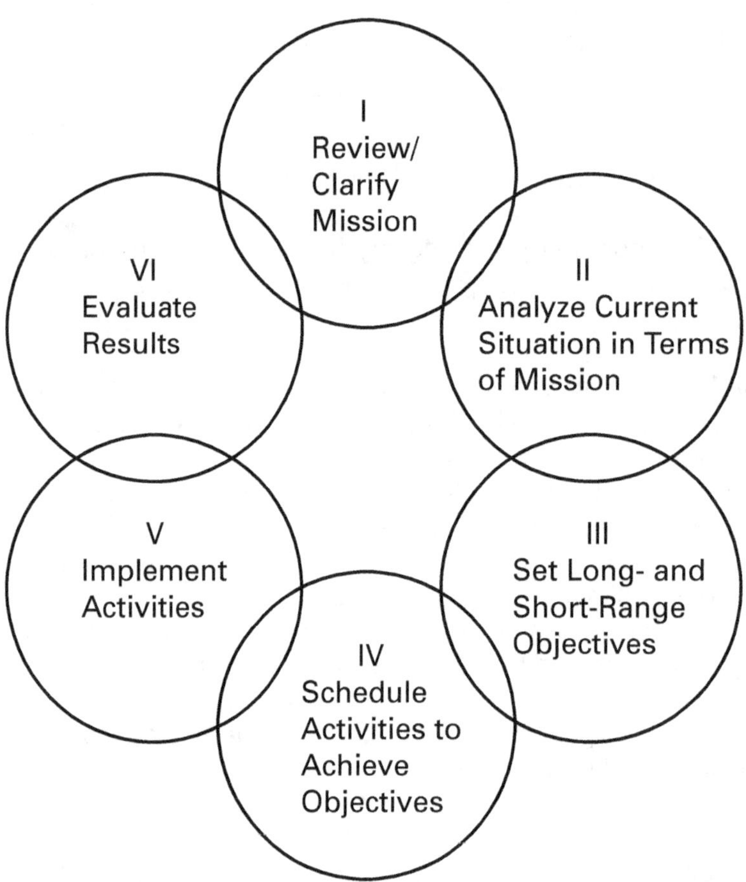

Step I: Review And/Or Clarify Your Mission.

Does your mission statement truly express your core values? If not, revise it. List 4 or 5 concrete steps you are willing to take to express your core values in your career. In other words, let the expression of your core values guide your performance improvement.

Step II: Analyze your current situation in terms of your mission. To start this process, ask yourself these questions:

1. What's my status today in terms of my mission?
2. What should I accomplish next?
3. Do I need special skills, help or resources to do this? If so, how can I develop and/or acquire them?
4. Do I have someone I trust to hold me accountable?

Step III: Set long- and short-range objectives for yourself.

Make sure your objectives are: 1) clearly related to your mission, 2) believable, and 3) challenging. Measure your results in terms of your mission. For example, choose standards that you want to meet in such metrics as quantity, cost effectiveness, impact on your organization, accuracy, completeness and quality.

It is important to make sure that your goals are challenging because achievement requires the improvement of skill. On the other hand, do not set goals that are so high you do not believe you can achieve them. It is better to set smaller goals that make you stretch—but are within reach—than to set goals that are so high you are sure to fail. Each time you achieve a goal, your confidence will grow and you can gradually set the bar higher and higher.

Also be sure to set a completion date for your objectives.

Step IV: Schedule the activities you need to take to achieve your objectives.

Make these a priority and do them before any other demands on your time. To help you achieve this, see the Ideal Work Week Exercise in this chapter. (Note: You can also find the Ideal Work Week Exercise in Appendix 1.)

Step V: Implement The Activities.

Make a commitment to yourself not to procrastinate. Remind yourself of your core values, your mission and your vision. Then just do it!
Step VI: Evaluate the results. Constantly assess what you do. You can't improve unless you know what you did well and what you did poorly. Ask for feedback from your manager, customers, and trusted friends and implement their suggestions.

Then repeat the cycle over and over!

Continuous Performance Improvement Exercises

The following exercises will help you achieve your goal to improve continuously—especially if you practice them regularly:

1. Ideal Work Week
2. Daily Checklist
3. Success Factor Development Journal

Exercise 1: The Ideal Work Week

The Ideal Work Week exercise helps your track your activities so you understand where your time is actually going.

To create it, begin by reviewing your appointment calendar for the last 30 to 60 days and writing down how you spent your time each day. One way to reconstruct your schedule is to analyze your office activities, such as the time you spent on paperwork or case preparation. Another way is to track your time for the next 30 days and then use this information to construct your ideal work week.

The more accurately and precisely you track your activities (such as hour by hour), the better you will understand where your time goes, what your priorities are, and how to be more effective and efficient with your time.

Once you have some data to work with, combine similar tasks into categories. For example, you could combine activities like reviewing applications and filling out tracking reports into one category named "administration."

Then calculate the amount of time you invest in each category and convert it to the average amount of time you spend each week in each category. For example:

Current Work Week	
Activity	Time
Laser Planning*	0.5
Administration	12.0
Training / Professional Development	1.0
Appointments	10.0
Appointments	6.0
Telephoning	2.0
Case Preparation	4.5
Fail Safe/Catch Up	1.0
Health	2.0
Misc.	21.0
Total	60.0

*Note: Laser Planning means setting aside 10 to 20 minutes each day to review your day's activities and to schedule appropriate time during the week to accomplish what needs to get done.

Convert the average number of hours you invest each week into the percentage it represents of your work week. Then graph your results in a pie chart. To do so, either use a spreadsheet application like Excel or simply draw a pie chart by hand.

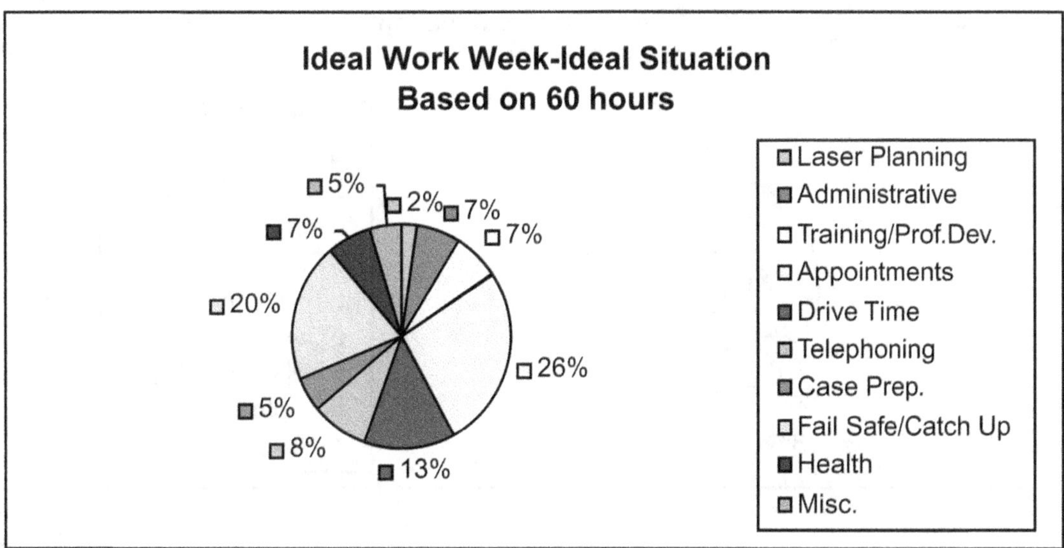

Now create an Ideal Work Week Schedule using the same categories as above. To decide what's ideal for you, you will need to determine the amount of sales activity that is required to achieve your production goals. (For a more detailed explanation of how to set and achieve your goals, refer to the Results Orientation Sales Factor in Chapter 6.)

Ideal Work Week Schedule	
Activity	Time
Laser Planning*	1.25
Administration	4.0
Training / Professional Development	4.0
Appointments	16.0
Appointments	8.0
Telephoning	5.0
Case Preparation	3.0
Fail Safe/Catch Up	12.0
Health	4.0
Misc.	2.75
Total	60.0

The next step is to turn your ideal work week into a graph:

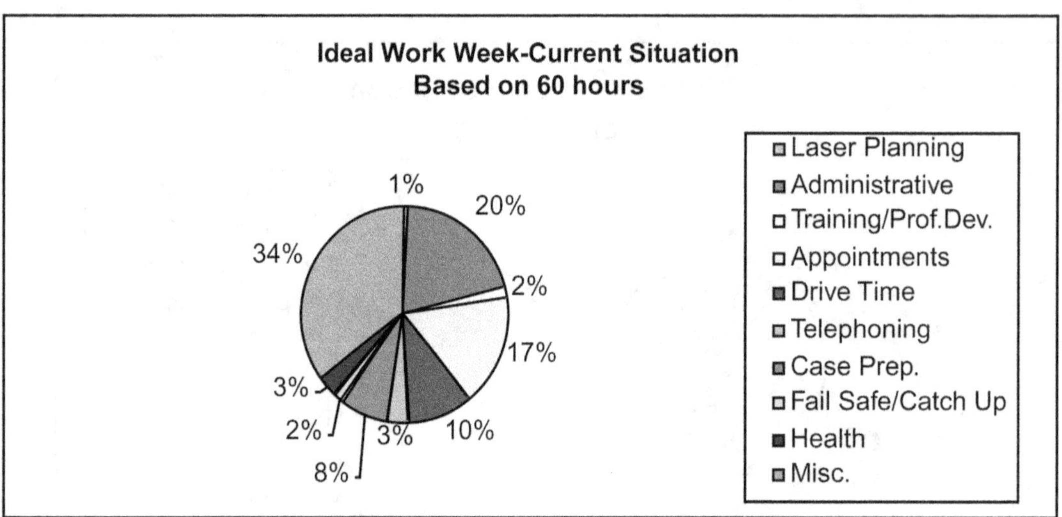

Then compare your Current Work Week allocation of time to your Ideal Work Week allocation of time. This will help you determine which categories of time you need to devote more attention to. Then plot your Ideal Work Week on an actual calendar. For example:

Sample Ideal Work Week (Copyright © 2009 Polaris One)

	Monday	Tuesday	Wednesday	Thursday	Friday	Saturday
7:00-7:15am	Laser Planning	Laser Planning	Laser Planning	Laser Planning	Laser Planning.	Optional Fail Safe Time
8:00 am	Administration	Telephone	Appointment 8-9	Telephone	Administration	Catch Up
9:00 am			Appointment 9:30-10:30			Administration
10:00 am	Training	Appointment 10:30-11:30		Appointment 10:30-11:30	Professional Development	Telephone
11:00 am	Meeting		Appointment 11-12			Planning Other
12:00 pm	Appointment 12-1	Appointment 12-1	Appointment 12:30-1:30	Appointment 12-1	Fail Safe Time	
1:00 pm		Appointment 1:30-2:30		Appointment 1:30-2:30	Catch Up	
2:00 pm	Appointment 1:30-2:30		Appointment 2-3		Administration	
3:00 pm		Appointment 3-4	Administration	Appointment 3-4	Personal	
4:00 pm	Appointment 4-5	Telephone			Get Ahead	
5:00 pm	Case Prep.	Gym	Case Prep.	Gym	Other	
6:00 pm						
7:00 pm	Open	Open	Open	Open	Open	

Time Summary

Laser Planning	1.25 hrs.	Telephoning:	5.00 hrs.
Administration	4.00 hrs.	Case Prep:	3.00 hrs.
Training/Professional Development	4.00 hrs.	Fail Safe/Catch up:	12.00 hrs.
Appointments	16.00 hrs.	Health:	4.00 hrs.

Finally, transfer your Ideal Work Week to your actual appointment calendar.

Commit yourself to closely following your Ideal Work Week schedule, treating it the same as you would an actual appointment with a client or prospect. For example, if during Laser Planning on Monday morning you determine that you need 45 minutes to prepare the Tom Smith case, then write in "Tom Smith" in the specific Case Preparation time block where you need to complete the work.

Finally, reward yourself for a job well done! Maintaining the discipline to adhere to your Ideal Work Week schedule will not only increase your bottom line, but it will also add more constructive hours to your day.

Exercise II: The Daily Checklist

The Daily Checklist Exercise will help you simplify the process of instituting continual performance improvement.

The first step is to type your mission statement in the Daily Checklist form on the following page so you will see it every day. Then print out enough copies of the form for each day of the week. (You can also find a copy of the form in Appendix 2.) Take a few minutes in the morning to think through and jot down what you plan to do that day and what you need in order to do it. Take a few minutes in the evening to evaluate how well you did and what you need to do better tomorrow in order to achieve your goals.

The Daily Checklist

Morning	Date/Time:
My mission:	
Considering my mission, what are my specific goals for today?	
What steps do I need to take to accomplish these goals?	
What skills/people/assistance do I need to carry this out?	

Evening	Date/Time:
How well did I do at implementing my specific goals for the day? What worked? What didn't?	
How can I improve tomorrow? What do I need to do next?	

Exercise III: The Success Factor Development Journal

One of the most effective tools you can use in your sales career is a personal journal. Writing helps us acquire new knowledge and synthesize it so it becomes part of us. It helps us discover what we really think and feel about a subject, and it helps us come up with insights that would otherwise have remained unconscious if we had not written them down.

Keeping a journal enables us to play with an idea, look at it from different angles, explore relationships, and analyze and synthesize. It also helps us set goals, evaluate how well we have achieved them, and determine the best steps to take next.

The simplest way to create a journal is to simply buy a three-ring binder and some paper. This way, it is easy to add and remove pages, as well as to incorporate extra information, such as the Daily Checklist form.

You can also print copies of the journal form provided in Appendix 3.

The Next Step

Now that you have developed your mission and vision statements, understand the personal psychology of sales success, and have acquired some tools you can use to implement the Continual Improvement Process, it is time to discover which sales success factors represent your strengths and which ones need further development.

Chapter 3   Sales Competency Self-Assessment

The Sales Competency Self-Assessment Questionnaire will help you rate your use of the core behaviors that represent how outstanding sales people use each of the 15 sales success factors. The results will tell you which factors and core behaviors are your strengths and which ones you should focus on for development.

Rating levels for the core behaviors	
1 = Novice	Uses **little or none** of this behavior Beginner's level of effectiveness Beginner's level of understanding
2 = Basic	Uses this behavior but in **a limited range of situation**s Some effectiveness Some understanding
3 = Capable	Uses this behavior in the **majority of situations** that require it Effective Good understanding
4 = Strength	Uses this behavior in **almost all situations** that require it Very effective Depth of understanding
5 = Expert	**Always** uses the behavior **where appropriate** Outstanding effectiveness Outstanding understanding

Questionnaire Directions

Read the description of each core behavior and decide which of the rating levels best describes your use of that core behavior. In the rating column to the right of the core behavior, circle the number of the level you have selected. Base your ratings on what you have actually done in past sales career experiences, not on what you think you might do in the future. If you have not yet had an opportunity to use a core behavior, circle "1" (Novice). After you are done, go on to the next section, which tells you how to score the questionnaire and profile your results.

The Sales Success Factors Self-Assessment Questionnaire

1. SHOWS SELF-DISCIPLINE Is persistent in work routines and in following through on customer relationships.		Rating
a. Follows through on commitments to self and others.		1 2 3 4 5
b. Sets priorities and systematizes routine work to assure that prime time can be spent on critical activities.		1 2 3 4 5
c. Focuses on the task at hand and does not allow self to be distracted from planned work activities.		1 2 3 4 5
d. Uses routine systems for getting the work done (e.g., systems for prospecting, maintaining customer relationships and handling administrative details).		1 2 3 4 5
e. Puts in the time necessary to get a job done right.		1 2 3 4 5

2. HAS SELF-CONFIDENCE Has an optimistic belief in own ability to succeed even in the face of challenging obstacles.		Rating
a. Takes on difficult and challenging assignments.		1 2 3 4 5
b. Is assured of own ability to bring situations under control.		1 2 3 4 5
c. Maintains composure in dealing with powerful people.		1 2 3 4 5
d. Moves beyond own comfort zone; conquers anxieties and personal blocks to achievement.		1 2 3 4 5
e. Takes setbacks in stride; recovers from disappointments.		1 2 3 4 5

3. **MAINTAINS SELF-CONTROL** Holds back an ineffective, spontaneous response to a situation and substitutes another, more effective, response in order to meet business needs.		**Rating**
a. Keeps own emotions from interfering with work.		1 2 3 4 5
b. Responds constructively in the face of rejection or attack.		1 2 3 4 5
c. Overcomes obstacles to sales success, such as call reluctance.		1 2 3 4 5
d. Rarely, if ever, develops negative stress—keeps stress at a level where it motivates, rather than frustrates.		1 2 3 4 5
e. Maintains stamina under continuing stress.		1 2 3 4 5

4. **ASSESSES SELF ACCURATELY** Is aware of own strengths and limitations.		**Rating**
a. Looks for feedback and new perspectives on self.		1 2 3 4 5
b. Is motivated by continuous learning and self-development.		1 2 3 4 5
c. Has the ability to target areas for personal change and growth.		1 2 3 4 5
d. Admits mistakes and personal weaknesses.		1 2 3 4 5
e. Knows personal capabilities and does not hesitate to ask for help from people who are more knowledgeable.		1 2 3 4 5

5. HAS A RESULTS ORIENTATION Has the resolve to set challenging goals and the persistence to achieve them in the face of obstacles.		Rating
a. Focuses on measurable, challenging goals and is disciplined in following through on action plans.		1 2 3 4 5
b. Shows a strong sense of urgency about solving problems and getting desired results.		1 2 3 4 5
c. Creates measures of excellence beyond those set by management.		1 2 3 4 5
d. Acts decisively to pursue opportunities that promise the best return on time and effort.		1 2 3 4 5
e. Focuses on profitable sales opportunities.		1 2 3 4 5

6. IS ADAPTABLE Modifies style and approach in order to achieve a specific objective in a given situation.		Rating
a. Explores different possibilities rather then just the obvious.		1 2 3 4 5
b. Decides what to do based on the situation.		1 2 3 4 5
c. Is willing to change own mind in the light of new evidence.		1 2 3 4 5
d. Is able to juggle multiple demands.		1 2 3 4 5
e. Changes plans or strategies when the initial approach does not work.		1 2 3 4 5

<table>
<tr><td colspan="2">7. QUESTIONS EFFECTIVELY
Follows a questioning strategy that leads to a complete mutual understanding of the problems that must be solved for the prospect to get the desired results.</td><td>Rating</td></tr>
<tr><td>a.</td><td>Formulates a questioning strategy to help customers discover and verbalize their needs.</td><td>1 2 3 4 5</td></tr>
<tr><td>b.</td><td>Asks questions that cause customers to analyze, evaluate, speculate or express their feelings.</td><td>1 2 3 4 5</td></tr>
<tr><td>c.</td><td>Listens carefully. When answers are unclear or do not contain required information, asks further clarifying questions.</td><td>1 2 3 4 5</td></tr>
<tr><td>d.</td><td>Pursues questioning until all needed answers are given.</td><td>1 2 3 4 5</td></tr>
<tr><td>e.</td><td>Asks for reasons behind answers and evidence to support apparent conclusions.</td><td>1 2 3 4 5</td></tr>
</table>

<table>
<tr><td colspan="2">8. APPLIES TARGETED PROBLEM SOLVING
Matches the priority problems in the prospect's situation with solutions that will exactly meet the client's needs.</td><td>Rating</td></tr>
<tr><td>a.</td><td>Identifies the cause and effect relationships in the prospect's problem situation.</td><td>1 2 3 4 5</td></tr>
<tr><td>b.</td><td>Recognizes evidence and impact of the prospect's problems.</td><td>1 2 3 4 5</td></tr>
<tr><td>c.</td><td>Peels back multiple layers of a problem.</td><td>1 2 3 4 5</td></tr>
<tr><td>d.</td><td>Identifies several solutions and weighs the value of each.</td><td>1 2 3 4 5</td></tr>
<tr><td>e.</td><td>Recommends solutions that will produce the desired results for the prospect.</td><td>1 2 3 4 5</td></tr>
</table>

9. **FOCUSES ON CUSTOMER SUCCESS** Relentlessly focuses on understanding and responding to the customer's needs.		**Rating**
a. Invests time and energy to understand the customer's total situation; becomes immersed in the customer's goals, needs and problems.		1 2 3 4 5
b. Helps customers clarify and prioritize their needs and expectations.		1 2 3 4 5
c. Is focused on helping customers succeed.		1 2 3 4 5
d. Acts as each customer's advocate within the company.		1 2 3 4 5
e. Helps customers think through how proposed solutions can best meet their needs.		1 2 3 4 5

10. **HAS INTERPERSONAL SENSITIVITY** Recognizes and responds to the feelings, attitudes and motivations of others.		**Rating**
a. Has the ability to see things from another's perspective.		1 2 3 4 5
b. Acknowledges the unique experiences, background and perspective of others.		1 2 3 4 5
c. Notices and adjusts own actions in response to others' verbal and non-verbal behavior (e.g., body language, tone of voice, innuendo).		1 2 3 4 5
d. Understands where another person's feelings are coming from and responds appropriately.		1 2 3 4 5
e. Recognizes the concerns and interests of others.		1 2 3 4 5

<table>
<tr><td colspan="2">11. GAINS COMMITMENT
Has the ability to convince others of an idea or course of action to effectively gain their support and get them to act accordingly.</td><td></td><td>Rating</td></tr>
<tr><td>a.</td><td>Creates and takes advantage of opportunities to gain credibility.</td><td></td><td>1 2 3 4 5</td></tr>
<tr><td>b.</td><td>Calculates the rational and emotional impact of own actions or words on others.</td><td></td><td>1 2 3 4 5</td></tr>
<tr><td>c.</td><td>Attracts the attention of others and communicates to them in a way they want to hear.</td><td></td><td>1 2 3 4 5</td></tr>
<tr><td>d.</td><td>Presents logical, fact-based data to motivate others to action.</td><td></td><td>1 2 3 4 5</td></tr>
<tr><td>e.</td><td>Shows others that a proposed action will bring about the solution to a problem and have a positive impact.</td><td></td><td>1 2 3 4 5</td></tr>
</table>

<table>
<tr><td colspan="2">12. HAS ENTREPRENEURIAL DRIVE
Is committed to the development of business opportunities and has the determination to overcome obstacles on the path to success.</td><td></td><td>Rating</td></tr>
<tr><td>a.</td><td>Takes pride in being a sales professional with a sense of mission about the work.</td><td></td><td>1 2 3 4 5</td></tr>
<tr><td>b.</td><td>Thrives on challenge; seeks out opportunities requiring some risk-taking and inventiveness to achieve a worthwhile goal.</td><td></td><td>1 2 3 4 5</td></tr>
<tr><td>c.</td><td>Focuses energy on continuous personal improvement.</td><td></td><td>1 2 3 4 5</td></tr>
<tr><td>d.</td><td>Takes initiative in finding creative solutions to client needs and new ways of doing business.</td><td></td><td>1 2 3 4 5</td></tr>
<tr><td>e.</td><td>Pursues new markets and greater levels of client service.</td><td></td><td>1 2 3 4 5</td></tr>
</table>

		Rating
13. USES KEY INFORMATION EFFECTIVELY Learns, knows and uses key information about own company and industry as well as the marketplace for the company's products.		
a. Gets information from many sources.		1 2 3 4 5
b. Knows the right person to contact and how to get things done in own company.		1 2 3 4 5
c. Knows features and customer benefits of company products and services.		1 2 3 4 5
d. Knows industry trends and what is happening with competitive products and services.		1 2 3 4 5
e. Knows the present needs and trends for the future in the marketplace for company products and services.		1 2 3 4 5

		Rating
14. INCREASES CUSTOMER VALUE Is able to leverage "high potential" customer relationships to create added value for customers and own business.		
a. Leverages sales to gain additional business.		1 2 3 4 5
b. Works to assure that existing customers continue to do business with own organization.		1 2 3 4 5
c. Maintains contact with clients; recognizes and acts upon business with own organization opportunities or problems.		1 2 3 4 5
d. Proactively and regularly brings to customers' attention the services and products that meet their needs.		1 2 3 4 5
e. Uses understanding of the customer to create a dramatically useful impact on the customer's organization.		1 2 3 4 5

15. BUILDS A TEAM Works to strengthen formal and informal relationships that can be called on to support the effort to achieve own sales career mission.		Rating
a. Builds long-term, in-depth relationships that can be leveraged for later work.		1 2 3 4 5
b. Gives directions and makes suggestions that help others maximize their potential and recognize options.		1 2 3 4 5
c. Provides task focus and direction and ensures that staff members understand performance standards.		1 2 3 4 5
d. Creates an environment where people can work together to meet organizational goals.		1 2 3 4 5
e. Promotes cooperation and collaboration between individuals and groups.		1 2 3 4 5

Scoring the Questionnaire

The score for each success factor is the total of the ratings for the core behaviors for that success factor. For example, if your ratings for the Self-Discipline success factor were...

1. SHOWS SELF-DISCIPLINE Is persistent in work routines and in following through on customer relationships.		Rating
a. Follows through on commitments to self and others.		1 2 3 **4** 5
b. Sets priorities and systematizes routine work to assure that prime time can be spent on critical activities.		1 **2** 3 4 5
c. Focuses on the task at hand and does not allow self to be distracted from planned work activities.		1 2 **3** 4 5
d. Uses routine systems for getting the work done (e.g., systems for prospecting, maintaining customer relationships and handling administrative details).		1 2 **3** 4 5
e. Puts in the time necessary to get a job done right.		1 2 3 **4** 5

...then you would add the underlined numbers.

```
     4
     2
     3
     3
    _4
    16
```

Your sales success factor score for Self-Discipline would be 16.

Once you have scored yourself on all of the sales success factors, enter your scores in the graph on the next page using a pen to draw a line up to your score for each factor.

Success Factors Profile

Success Factor	5	10	15	20	25
Example Answer 16					
1. Shows Self-Discipline					
2. Has Self-Confidence					
3. Maintains Self-Control					
4. Assesses Self Accurately					
5. Has a Results Orientation					
6. Is Adaptable					
7. Questions & Listens Effectively					
8. Applies Targeted Problem Solving					
9. Focuses on Customer Success					
10. Has Interpersonal Sensitivity					
11. Gains Commitment					
12. Has Entrepreneurial Drive					
13. Uses Key Information Effectively					
14. Increases Customer Value					
15. Builds a Team					

<table><tr><td>Chapter 4</td><td></td></tr></table>

Overview of the 15 Sales Success Factors

Now that you know which of the core behaviors of outstanding sales people represent your strengths and which ones need more development, it's time to go to work!

Each of the next four chapters focuses in depth on one area of mastery (Self, Sales Process, Customer Relationships, and Own Business) and the personal competencies that belong to it. Working through each of your weak competencies step-by-step will give you the opportunity to understand, practice and incorporate its skills, habits and thought processes into your own life. You goal is to leverage your strengths and manage your weaknesses.

For best results, follow this five-step process:

1. **Recognize the competency.** The first step is to identify and label each competency as superior salespeople actually use it in their careers.

2. **Understand the competency.** The second step is to describe each competency in your own words and integrate it into your way of thinking about how to create a successful sales career.

3. **Clearly assess yourself in relation to the competency.** The third step is to create an accurate picture of your ability to use each competency on the job so you can identify specific areas for self-improvement.

4. **Practice using the competency.** The fourth step is to develop your ability to use the competency by practicing the appropriate skills and attitudes in low-risk, experiential activities.

5. *Apply the competency on the job and obtain feedback from others so you can improve your performance.* The fifth step is to apply the competency within the normal complexities of your day-to-day activities, evaluate your success, identify areas for improvement, and start the cycle again.

To help you accomplish the five-step development process, the exercises in Chapters 5 through 8 draw on two special tools: Affirmations and Visualization.

Affirmations

An affirmation is a statement that you repeat in your mind or write down on paper over and over to yourself. Affirmations focus your inner thoughts and conscious efforts on transformation. They help you replace old mental patterns and self-defeating thoughts that are blocking you with more positive, more effective thoughts. Once the new belief becomes part of your subconscious mind, your actions, emotions and experiences will begin to reflect the change in your daily life.

Affirmations should always be stated in positive terms in the present tense—as though whatever you are affirming has already occurred. When you are repeating the affirmation to yourself (or writing it), visualize how happy and successful you feel now that your goal has been achieved. For example:

> *I have confidence in my ability to handle sales objections and concerns. I eagerly anticipate what they might be and am confident I will help my clients discover for themselves the solutions and answers that best fit their needs.*

If you write an affirmation that is tentative and stated in the future, it loses all of its power. Compare the following affirmation with the one above, and you will see what I mean:

> **Weak Affirmation:** *I hope to be able to handle any sales objections and concerns that I may receive in the future. I will do my best, and perhaps succeed someday, in helping my clients discover their own solutions and the answers that best fit their needs..*

Working With Affirmations

In working with affirmations, your objective is to get to the place where you know and feel that you have already achieved your goal—in the present moment. The most effective way to do this is to write down your affirmations and look at them frequently throughout the day. This helps to clarify them and make them concrete. Place your affirmations in places where you will see them often. For example, write them on a sticky note and place them on a bathroom mirror at home, on the edge of your computer screen, or in your daily planner or journal.

Visualization

Visualization is the process of creating pictures in your mind to gain greater understanding of an issue, obtain information about it, or achieve something you desire, such as increased sales. The key to making visualization effective is to incorporate strong, positive emotions into your picture and to use all of your senses (sight, sound, touch, smell, and hearing) as though you were watching or participating in a vivid movie of your life.

Athletes have used visualization successfully for years to practice winning races and garner gold medals. Before a race, they will spend time seeing themselves easily running around the track, moving into the best position, outpacing their competitors, and breaking through the barrier first. In fact, many athletes credit this process with their success during the actual race.

In recent years, neuroscientists have conducted research that backs up this assertion. They have discovered that the same areas light up in the brain when we physically perform an act as when we simply imagine that we are performing an act. In other words, the brain can't tell the difference!

So use the power of your mind to focus on the positive results you want to achieve, not to focus on your mistakes. See yourself—smiling, happy and self-confident—stepping to the front of the room to accept the prize vacation for being the top salesperson in your company. The more you concentrate on positive outcomes and emotions, the faster you will experience them in your career.

Visualization Steps

Follow these steps to visualize successfully:

1. Go to a quiet, comfortable place where you will be undisturbed for at least 30 minutes.

2. Close your eyes and take a few deep breaths. Now tense every muscle you can in your body and hold for a few seconds. Then release the tension and take a few more deep breaths.

3. Now think about the competency you want to acquire or improve. Create a scene in your mind in which you are using this competency easily, successfully, without hesitation. Where are you? Who are you with? What is happening? How do you feel now that you have completely integrated this competency into your arsenal of sales tools? How are your experiences different? What new levels of success have you achieved in your career?

4. Use as many senses (sight, smell, taste, sound, touch) and positive emotions as you can to envision the details. In particular, focus on how wonderful you feel for having acquired this competency.

When you have finished visualizing, take a few deep breaths and open your eyes, refreshed and ready to continue your day.

The Framework Of Chapters 5 Through 8

Chapters 5 through 8 take you through each competency using a set process built around the five-step program described at the beginning of this chapter.

To help you **Recognize the Competency,** you will read a list of descriptions that characterize people who share the competency and a list of descriptions that characterize people who lack the competency.

To help you **Understand the Competency,** Exercise 1 asks you to recognize it in others. You do this by observing people around you and choosing someone who clearly demonstrates the competency. Then you write down why you believe this is true. Exercise 1 also asks you to write a definition of the competency in your own words, which further reinforces your understanding of it from your own point of view.

To help you **Assess Yourself in Relation to the Competency,** Exercise 2 asks you to describe in your own words how you could use the competency in your life to increase success in your sales career.

To help you **Practice the Competency** in a low-risk, experiential way, Exercise 3 asks you to **create your own positive affirmations** for it. It then asks you to **create a mental picture, or visualization,** of yourself successfully using this competency in your own career. The final step is to **create a daily practice** in which you focus on your affirmation, set your intent, and visualize yourself—happy, successful, and self-confident—using this competency in your sales career.

It is important to do these exercises slowly, carefully, thoughtfully and consistently. Recognizing how you use the competencies and changing your emotions and habits of thought will take time and effort. Therefore, make a daily habit of clarifying and setting your intentions, repeating your affirmations, visualizing positive outcomes, and writing in your journal. You will probably not change overnight, but you WILL change if you put in the time and effort it requires.

Case Studies:

To further reinforce your understanding of each competency, the book also includes numerous **Case Studies** that illustrate how others have come to recognize their challenges with individual competencies and learned how to understand, practice and fine-tune them until they became a natural part of themselves.

Recommended Tools:

To help you **Apply the Competency on the Job**, we recommend that you make extensive use of the **Ideal Work Week Exercise** (Appendix 1), the **Daily Checklist** (Appendix 2), and the **Sales Success Factors Journal** (Appendix 3).

The Sales Success Development Plan:

To further reinforce each sales success factor, we have created the Sales Success Development Plan (Appendix 4), which consists of a simple form you can print out and put in your Success Factors Journal. The form gives you a place on which to write down your goals, action items, potential obstacles, sources of help, and measurements/time frames. Using this tool regularly will greatly facilitate your skill with each success factor.

The results of putting these into practice will be well worth your effort!

Mastery of Self

Take a moment to reflect upon the best bosses or managers you have ever worked with. What traits did they possess that you admired? Would your business success be enhanced by emulating their positive managerial traits?

While you will almost certainly have different bosses throughout your career, you will never escape yourself. This is why the most important manager you will ever have is you. By setting goals and applying the tools you need to manage yourself and your life effectively, you will give yourself the leadership necessary to succeed in your career.

With dedication and practice, you will develop the four main competencies consistently found in top achievers: Shows Self Discipline, Has Self Confidence, Maintains Self Control, and Assesses Self Accurately.

Sales Success Factor 1: Shows Self-Discipline

Self-disciplined sales people are persistent in their work routines. They follow through on customer relationships, record their progress, and report to a manager, coach or mentor.

Highly self-disciplined salespeople:
* Follow through on commitments to self and others.
* Set priorities and systematize routine work so they can spend their prime time on critical activities.
* Focus on the task at hand and do not allow themselves to be distracted from their planned work activities.
* Use routine systems for getting the work done (e.g., systems for prospecting, maintaining customer relationships and handling administrative details).
* Put in the time necessary to get the job done right.

Salespeople who LACK self-discipline:
* Are easily distracted.
* Are disorganized in their work.
* Have no established work plans or routines.
* Forget assignments and miss appointments and deadlines.
* Fail to track their sales activities and results.

Exercise 1: Understanding the Self-Discipline Competency

To get a better understanding of how this competency works in your life, try this exercise.

Understanding Self–Discipline
Write the name of a person you know who possesses this sales success factor: ____ Describe the evidence for choosing this individual.
Write your own definition of the Self-Discipline sales success factor.

Exercise 2: Applying the Self-Discipline Competency

Now describe how you can use this competency to help you create a successful sales career.

Understanding Self–Discipline
How I can apply this competency in my life

Exercise 3: Practicing the Self-Discipline Competency

Now that you understand more about this competency and have a clearer picture of how it might work in your sales career, it is time to practice what you have learned by creating specific affirmations for it and spending time visualizing that it is already creating success in your career.

An example of an affirmation focused on self-discipline is:

- Because I am stick-to-itive in my work habits, my customers can count on me to follow through to see that I meet every one of my commitments to them.

If you scored low on certain behaviors in this category of the self-assessment test, try writing an affirmation for each one. For example:

- During the workday, I focus on critical tasks and don't allow myself to be distracted by trivia.
- I set work priorities and stick to them.
- My systematic way of planning my workweek is paying off in productivity.

Now write your own affirmations in the space below. Remember to keep them short and simple and to phrase them in the present tense as though you were describing your current reality. When you are done, sign your statement.

<table>
<tr><td>My Self-Discipline Affirmations</td></tr>
<tr><td>I, _______________________________ declare that the following statements are true about me:

Signed: _______________________________</td></tr>
</table>

Create A Daily Practice

Now that you have written and visualized your affirmations, the next step is to practice them regularly until they become second nature to you. Adhering to the following steps will greatly increase your ability to incorporate and apply the competency successfully in your life.

Set your intention, affirm and visualize. Take a few moments at the beginning and ending of each day to read through your affirmations, set your intention to incorporate them into your life, and visualize yourself easily and joyfully applying them in your sales career.

Write in your Daily Checklist and *Sales Success Factor Development Journal.* Make a few notes in the Morning/Evening section of your Daily Checklist (Appendix 2) and write down any additional thoughts that occur to you in your journal (Appendix 3).

Review your Sales Success Factors Development Plan. Be sure to create a Sales Success Factors Development Plan (Appendix 4) to help you develop this competency. Then review it daily to make sure you are on track.

Reassess, Reward, Revise, And Repeat

After practicing your affirmations for a few weeks, reassess how you are doing on the core behaviors of this competency. If you feel that you now use all aspects of the core behaviors effectively, reward yourself. If you need more work, write a new affirmation to target the core behaviors that are still weak. Then begin the cycle again.

Case Study: Creating An Ideal Workweek[tm]

Thomas was similar to many other advisors I work with. Although he was moderately successful in sales, many other associates with similar backgrounds and experience sold much more than he did. Thomas realized that his colleagues' practices were at a higher level than his, and he worked hard to achieve similar results. He took pride in the fact that he was a lifelong learner, an avid reader, attended all of his companies' trainings, and was continuously working to complete a multitude of industry designations. So what was missing? Clearly, knowledge alone was not the answer.

After observing Thomas for a while, I realized that he had poor organization and time management skills, which often stem from a lack of self-discipline.

I asked him to go back and track the way he had spent his time over the last three months on both business and non-business activities (e.g., administration, telephoning for appointments, case preparation, seeing clients, prospecting, personal errands, water cooler talk, etc.). After he had categorized his time, I asked him to calculate what percentage of it he was investing in each category. The results shocked him because they demonstrated that he was investing little quality time on the continued growth of his practice.

I then showed Thomas how to create an Ideal Work Week™ (see Appendix 1). In the beginning, he found it challenging to develop the self-discipline necessary to convert his ideals from paper to reality; however, the positive results he achieved soon took his business to the next level.

Here are some additional suggestions for working with this sales success factor:

Suggestions for Working with the Self-Discipline Competency

1. Observe a salesperson whose self-discipline you admire. Talk with this person about his or her attitudes toward work. Ask to see the tools that he or she uses to manage time, administrative activities and client follow-up.
2. Use a planning calendar to set priorities and to plan and record your daily and monthly activities. Hold yourself accountable to your plan.
3. Plan an effective office routine and make it a habit. Begin work early every day and aim for creating a common pattern for each week. Some people do this by planning an ideal work-week schedule.
4. Keep your office and desk neat, well organized, and free of distractions. Make a place for everything and keep everything in its place.
5. Say "no" to distractions.
6. In your Success Factor Development Journal, write about some common "time wasters" in your daily schedule, then create a plan to eliminate them. Use the extra time to devote to activities that promise the best return on your time and effort.
7. When you catch yourself being self-disciplined, give yourself some credit! Take the time to experience how good you feel about what you have done and encourage yourself to do it again. Record the experience in your Success Factor Development Journal.
8. Think of some times in the past when you have shown self-discipline. Try to identify common elements in those experiences. Seek opportunities for similar experiences in the future.

9. Become aware of your self-talk and make an effort to eliminate any negative thoughts that erode your discipline. Consciously substitute one of your affirmations and repeat it over and over instead.

Sales Success Factor 2: Has Self-Confidence

Self-confidant people have an optimistic belief in their own ability to succeed even in the face of challenging obstacles.

Self-confident salespeople:
- Take on difficult and challenging assignments.
- Are sure of their own ability to bring situations under control.
- Maintain composure in dealing with powerful people.
- Consciously take steps to move beyond their comfort zones.
- Conquer their anxieties and personal blocks to achievement.
- Take setbacks in stride and recover quickly from disappointments.

Salespeople who LACK self-confidence:
- Give up easily in the face of disagreement or rejection, experience call reluctance, and fail to answer objections.
- Are willing to compromise their values rather than take a stand on what they believe is right.
- Blame others for their problems rather than taking personal responsibility for them. (It's always the fault of the home office, delivery or someone in the office.)
- Avoid risks. They are reluctant to try new ideas because they are afraid of failing, and they won't volunteer answers because they are afraid of being wrong.

Exercise 1: Understanding the Self-Confidence Competency

To get a better understanding of how this competency works in your life, try this exercise.

Understanding Self-Confidence
Write the name of a person you know who possesses this sales success factor: ____ Describe the evidence for choosing this individual.
Write your own definition of the Self-Confidence sales success factor.

Exercise 2: Applying the Self-Confidence Competency

Now describe how you can use this competency to help you create a successful sales career.

How I can apply this competency in my life

Exercise 3: Practicing the Self-Confidence Competency

Now that you understand more about this competency and have a clearer picture of how it might work in your sales career, it is time to practice what you have learned by creating specific affirmations for it and spending time visualizing that it is already creating success in your career.

An example of an affirmation focused on developing self-confidence is:
- Each day I enjoy moving beyond my comfort zone and conquering my anxieties and personal blocks to achievement.

If you scored particularly low on certain behaviors in this category of the self- assessment test, try writing an affirmation for each one. For example:
- I welcome difficult and challenging assignments.
- I feel comfortable and look for the opportunity to work with the top decision makers in my clients' companies.
- I will continue to move ahead in my career in spite of an occasional setback or disappointment.

Now write your own affirmations in the space below. Remember to keep them short and simple and to phrase them in the present tense as though you were describing your current reality. When you are done, sign your statement.

Self-Confidence Affirmations

I, _________________________________ declare that the following statements are true about me:

Signed: _________________________________

Create A Daily Practice

Now that you have written and visualized your affirmations, the next step is to practice them regularly until they become second nature to you. Adhering to the following steps will greatly increase your ability to incorporate and apply the competency successfully in your life.

Set your intention, affirm and visualize. Take a few moments at the beginning and ending of each day to read through your affirmations, set your intention to incorporate them into your life, and visualize yourself easily and joyfully applying them in your sales career.

Write in your Daily Checklist and *Sales Success Factor Development Journal*. Make a few notes in the Morning/Evening section of your Daily Checklist (Appendix 2) and write down any additional thoughts that occur to you in your journal (Appendix 3).

Review your Sales Success Factors Development Plan. Be sure to create a Sales Success Factors Development Plan (Appendix 4) to help you develop this competency. Then review it daily to make sure you are on track.

Reassess, Reward, Revise, And Repeat

After practicing your affirmations for a few weeks, reassess how you are doing on the core behaviors of this competency. If you feel that you now use all aspects of the core behaviors effectively, reward yourself. If you need more work, write a new affirmation to target the core behaviors that are still weak. Then begin the cycle again

Case Study: Expanding belief boundaries

For Sarah, the fact that she had survived her first few years in sales was a miracle. But it did not surprise anyone else who knew her because her track record proved she could succeed at anything she put her mind to. Why didn't Sarah recognize this fact about herself?

We each operate within our own belief systems about what we perceive our abilities to be and what we believe is possible for us to achieve and accomplish. To prove the point, think about a time when you accomplished a goal you knew was in the realm of possibility for you. Now think of a goal you failed to accomplish because you knew it was out of your reach. How did the results differ? How did your emotions change as you thought about each example?

Our inner beliefs control all of our actions, attitudes, abilities, and habits. We will never act in a way that is inconsistent with those deeply held inner beliefs. Therefore, to expand our results, we must expand our thinking and our belief boundaries.

The sales profession offers us many more opportunities to fail than to succeed. None of us closes every sale we ask for or get appointments with everyone we want to get in front of. It is important to acknowledge this and to maintain a positive attitude in spite of it. This is because our attitude and beliefs about our ability to succeed profoundly impact our behaviors and sales success.

It's been said that we become what we think about most of the time. If this is true, what thoughts play out in your head each day? Are they mostly positive or negative? Are they self-affirming or self-destructive? To answer these questions, stop what you are doing periodically throughout the day and *listen in* to your self-talk. You may be surprised by what you hear.

I suggested to Sarah that she begin to keep a Success Journal™. This meant that every evening she began to take a few minutes to reflect upon her success that day. This included anything that she felt good about: big or small, it didn't matter. Over time, she developed a deep inner belief in herself and her abilities and her self-image and attitudes changed for the better. The more positive she felt, the better the sales results she experienced.

Keeping a Success Journal is easy to do and doesn't require much time, yet it can yield profound results.

Case Study: Overcoming A Negative View Of Selling

Self-confidence and self-esteem are critical sales success factors. They don't come in a one size fits all format, though; each of us has them to a different degree. To whatever extent we grade ourselves in self-confidence and self-esteem, improvements in these areas can have a disproportional impact on our sales.

Let me tell you about another sales executive named Seth. Seth had been scheduling an adequate number of appointments each week, with about 25% coming from referrals. Yet his closing ratio was only 1 out of 6 (16.6%) compared to the industry average of 1 out of 3 (33.3%). So what was his problem? After working with him for a while, I discovered that he had a very negative view of selling. His attitude came from many firsthand experiences with inept, non-caring salespeople who seemed to say, "I must make this sale because it's good for me."

As we worked together over the next few weeks, Seth came to realize that his negative view of selling was eroding his self-esteem and self-confidence; worst of all, he was unconsciously communicating this attitude to his prospects.

Once Seth realized that he was actually providing a very valuable service that helped his prospects solve problems and achieve their goals, his attitude changed 180 degrees. Today he feels proud of the work he does and approaches prospects with enthusiasm and confidence. As a result, Seth's closing ratio has dramatically improved and continues to get better and better.

Here are some additional suggestions for working with this sales success factor:

Suggestions for Working with the Self-Confidence Competency

1. Once you are committed to an action, just do it instead of reexamining every move.
2. Before your next customer contact, spend some time creating a mental picture of yourself performing successfully and getting the results you want.
3. If a prospect refuses to give you an appointment, don't take it personally. Some people will reject you for reasons totally unrelated to what you do or say. Move on to the next person on your list.
4. When you get good results, take time to praise yourself and feel good about it.
5. Keep a record of your sales accomplishments in your Success Factor Development Journal. Review the journal periodically to support your self-image as a person who is successful.
6. No matter how hard we try, we sometimes make mistakes. If your customer or colleague becomes angry, allow him or her to vent while remaining composed yourself. Listen carefully, without being defensive, and allow the situation to wind down until you can proceed with a reasonable, logical conversation.

> **Suggestions for Working with the Self-Confidence Competency, continued**
>
> 7. Devote some time to learning techniques that will help you deal successfully with confrontation.
> 8. Seek out people who handle confrontation well, such as a senior sales representative, an account manager or a group sales manager. Ask them how they acted when they had to take a tough stand. What steps did they take to clarify the problem and resolve it? How did they follow up?
> 9. Put yourself into new situations by setting aside a block of time each month to do something you have never done before. Keep notes about the activity (and your feelings) in your journal.
> 10. Think about times in your past when you felt self-confident. What elements are common to these memories? Seek out opportunities for similar experiences in the future.
> 11. Become aware of your self-talk and resolve to eliminate any negative thoughts that erode your self-confidence.
> 12. Recall how you learned specific skills (riding a bike, public speaking). Use the process to help you feel more confident when faced with a new learning challenge.

Sales Success Factor 3: Maintains Self-Control

Self-controlled sales people hold back ineffective, spontaneous responses to situations and substitute other, more effective, responses in order to meet business needs.

Salespeople with high scores in self-control:
- Keep their own emotions from interfering with work.
- Respond constructively in the face of rejection or attack.
- Overcome obstacles to sales success, such as call reluctance.
- Rarely, if ever, develop negative stress. They keep stress at a level where it motivates, rather than frustrates, them.
- Maintain stamina under continuing stress.

Salespeople who LACK self-control:
- React impulsively to stressful situations.
- Are likely to become angry, depressed, or agitated when faced with stress on the job.
- Get involved in inappropriate situations because they can't resist temptation.
- Respond to problems in a non-constructive way, especially in stressful situations.

Exercise 1: Understanding the Self-Control Competency

To get a better understanding of how this competency works in your life, try this exercise.

<table>
<tr><td>Understanding Self–Control</td></tr>
<tr><td>Write the name of a person you know who possesses this sales success factor:

____

Describe the evidence for choosing this individual.

</td></tr>
<tr><td>Write your own definition of the Self-Control sales success factor.

</td></tr>
</table>

Exercise 2: Applying the Self-Control Competency

Now describe how you can use this competency to help you create a successful sales career.

<table>
<tr><td>How I can apply this competency in my life</td></tr>
<tr><td>

</td></tr>
</table>

Exercise 3: Practicing the Self-Control Competency

Now that you understand more about the self-control competency and have a clearer picture of how it might work in your sales career, it is time to practice what you have learned by creating specific affirmations for it and spending time visualizing that it is already creating success in your career.

An example of an affirmation focused on self-control is:
- I think twice and respond positively when something negative or aggravating comes up in the course of my work.

If you scored particularly low on certain behaviors in this category of the self-assessment test, try writing an affirmation for each one. For example:
- I respond to stressful situations by striving to reduce the stress for everyone involved.
- I am able to control my emotions and keep them from interfering with the achievement of my objectives.

Now write your own affirmations in the space below. Remember to keep them short and simple and to phrase them in the present tense as though you were describing your current reality. When you are done, sign your statement.

Self-Control Affirmations

I, _________________________________ declare that the following statements are true about me:

Signed: _______________________________

Create A Daily Practice

Now that you have written and visualized your affirmations, the next step is to practice them regularly until they become second nature to you. Adhering to the following steps will greatly increase your ability to incorporate and apply the competency successfully in your life.

Set your intention, affirm and visualize. Take a few moments at the beginning and ending of each day to read through your affirmations, set your intention to incorporate them into your life, and visualize yourself easily and joyfully applying them in your sales career.

Write in your Daily Checklist and *Sales Success Factor Development Journal*. Make a few notes in the Morning/Evening section of your Daily Checklist (Appendix 2) and write down any additional thoughts that occur to you in your journal (Appendix 3).

Review your Sales Success Factors Development Plan. Be sure to create a Sales Success Factors Development Plan (Appendix 4) to help you develop this competency. Then review it daily to make sure you are on track.

Reassess, Reward, Revise, And Repeat

After practicing your affirmations for a few weeks, reassess how you are doing on the core behaviors of this competency. If you feel that you now use all aspects of the core behaviors effectively, reward yourself. If you need more work, write a new affirmation to target the core behaviors that are still weak. Then begin the cycle again.

Case Study: Listening carefully before responding

There's an old adage that states: "What gets rewarded gets repeated." Jason's reward was that he took pride in his ability to come back with a quick response to any objection a prospect could hurl at him. The only problem was that when he did so, he often turned off his prospects because they felt he wasn't listening to their concerns. For Jason, it was a matter of winning the battle but losing the war. This behavior also extended to the people he worked with in his office. After his closing ratio began to deteriorate substantially, he finally asked me for help.

It didn't take me long to hone in on Jason's weakness in listening to his prospects' concerns and issues. I began by asking him to write down all of the objections he commonly got from his prospects, especially the ones that caused him to have a knee-jerk reaction and lose control of his customer/prospect focus. Next, I had him write out thoughtful answers to those objections and practice giving them as his responses.

I told Jason that one of the most important steps he could take when confronted with an objection was to give 100% of his attention to *listening* to what his prospect was actually saying instead of thinking up a response. To be sure he clearly understood his prospect's point of view, I told him to paraphrase what his prospect had said and ask if this was correct. After receiving confirmation of this, I told him to respond to his prospect with a solution tailored to fit his prospect's specific needs.

My final suggestion to Jason was to debrief himself soon after he had left the appointment. To do this, I told him to replay the appointment in his mind. What elements had gone well? If he could do it all over again, what would he do differently? Did he encounter any new objections? How well did he think he had answered the objections that he had prepared in advance? In the future, could he answer one or more of these objections before the prospect brought it up?

By investing a small amount of time with pre-call preparation and planning and then acting as his own Monday morning quarterback following the appointment, I showed Jason how he could reap huge returns. (And you can, too.)

Case Study: Obtaining Referrals

 Sally had a different problem: She struggled to obtain referrals. She did her prospecting homework and consistently added a more than adequate supply of new prospect names to her call list. So why didn't she obtain more referrals? In her case, two reasons surfaced: lack of belief in her services and fear. She dreaded making the calls because she was afraid that by asking for referrals she would somehow jeopardize her good relationship with her clients. And she failed to see the value she delivered to her clients because in her mind, she was simply doing her job as a financial services professional.

One of the problems was that she had never learned the right way to ask for referrals. I suggested that she begin by asking her clients if they were satisfied with her services and had benefited from their work together. When she did so, their positive, heartfelt responses completely surprised her.

I then suggested that she simply ask for the names of other people who, like them, could benefit from her ideas and her approach to helping people achieve their financial and protection goals. To prepare, I asked her to write out a script she could use for this purpose. I instructed her to practice the script until it sounded natural to her and she was completely comfortable with it. Finally, I asked her to keep a record of all of her referral attempts and results.

Sally began to see positive results in the very first week that she used this approach. Ironically, even though she still needs to cold call to fill in the gaps, she doesn't mind doing this as much as she did before because her new-found confidence and positive attitude about the value of her services has spilled over to every aspect of her practice!

Here are some additional suggestions for working with this sales success factor:

<table>
<tr><td colspan="2">Suggestions for Working with the Self-Control Competency</td></tr>
<tr><td>1.</td><td>Show common courtesy to the office staff, no matter what frustrating mistakes they may have made.</td></tr>
<tr><td>2.</td><td>Keep your cool when rejected or attacked.</td></tr>
<tr><td>3.</td><td>Move ahead to the next call, no matter how badly you were turned down on the last one.</td></tr>
<tr><td>4.</td><td>Have plenty of prospects, so that if one rejects your approach you can comfortably move on to the next.</td></tr>
<tr><td>5.</td><td>Reflect on self-control in your Success Factor Development Journal. If you do not know that you are losing it, you will not be able to recognize it. Make a list of all the things that cause you to lose your self-control and write out a strategy to deal with these triggers the next time they occur. Be sure to share your strategies with someone who can offer additional insights and suggestions.</td></tr>
</table>

Suggestions for Working with the Self-Control Competency, continued

6. Identify someone whose self-control you admire. When you find that you are about to lose your own self-control, take a moment (silently count to ten) and ask yourself how your role model would handle this situation. Then tailor your reactions accordingly.

7. In your Success Factor Development Journal, write about some past experiences in which you dealt well with failure or disappointment. How were you able to overcome your negative feelings and move ahead? Apply what you learned from those experiences to help you handle your current frustrations.

8. Reduce your stress through physical activity or some type of conscious relaxation such as meditation, yoga or taking a bath.

Sales Success Factor 4: Assesses Self Accurately

Sales people who can assess themselves accurately are aware of their own strengths and limitations.

Salespeople who assess themselves accurately:
- Actively look for feedback and new perspectives on themselves.
- Are motivated by continuous learning and self-development.
- Have the ability to target areas for personal change and growth.
- Admit their mistakes and personal weaknesses.
- Know their personal capabilities and do not hesitate to ask for help from people who are more knowledgeable than they are.

Salespeople who LACK the ability to assess themselves accurately:
- Exaggerate their own value and contribution.
- Cannot admit their mistakes.
- Are enraged by criticism and reject it even when it is valid.
- Will not ask for help even if they are over their head in dealing with a customer problem.

Exercise 1: Understanding the Accurate Self-Assessment Competency

To get a better understanding of how this competency works in your life, try this exercise.

Understanding Accurate Self-Assessment
Write the name of a person you know who possesses this sales success factor: ______________________________________   Describe the evidence for choosing this individual.
Write your own definition of the Accurate Self-Assessment sales success factor.

Exercise 2: Applying the Accurate Self-Assessment Competency

Now describe how you can use this competency to help you create a successful sales career.

How I can apply this competency in my life

Exercise 3: Practicing the Accurate Self-Assessment Competency

Now that you understand more about this competency and have a clearer picture of how it might work in your sales career, it is time to practice what you have learned by creating specific affirmations for it and spending time visualizing that it is already creating success in your career.

An example of an affirmation focused on accurate self-assessment is:
- I am aware of my own strengths and limitations and approach my daily tasks and responsibilities accordingly.

If you scored particularly low on certain behaviors in this category of the self-assessment test, try writing an affirmation for each one. For example:

- I am willing to admit my own mistakes and personal weaknesses.
- I eagerly ask for help from others who are skilled in the activities where I am weak.
- To identify the areas where I need help improving my performance, I actively seek feedback.

Now write your own affirmations in the space below. Remember to keep them short and simple and to phrase them in the present tense as though you were describing your current reality. When you are done, sign your statement.

Accurate Self-Assessment Affirmations

I, _________________________________ declare that the following statements are true about me:

Signed: _________________________________

Create a daily practice

Now that you have written and visualized your affirmations, the next step is to practice them regularly until they become second nature to you. Adhering to the following steps will greatly increase your ability to incorporate and apply the competency successfully in your life.

Set your intention, affirm and visualize. Take a few moments at the beginning and ending of each day to read through your affirmations, set your intention to incorporate them into your life, and visualize yourself easily and joyfully applying them in your sales career.

Write in your Daily Checklist and *Sales Success Factor Development Journal*. Make a few notes in the Morning/Evening section of your Daily Checklist (Appendix 2) and write down any additional thoughts that occur to you in your journal (Appendix 3).

Review your Sales Success Factors Development Plan. Be sure to create a Sales Success Factors Development Plan (Appendix 4) to help you develop this competency. Then review it daily to make sure you are on track.

Reassess, Reward, Revise, And Repeat

After practicing your affirmations for a few weeks, reassess how you are doing on the core behaviors of this competency. If you feel that you now use all aspects of the core behaviors effectively, reward yourself. If you need more work, write a new affirmation to target the core behaviors that are still weak. Then begin the cycle again.

Case Study: Getting feedback from others

It is important to assess our strengths and weaknesses accurately—both in our business and in our personal lives. Unfortunately, we are often too close to a situation to see it realistically. This sometimes leads us to discount our strengths and overlook our shortcomings.

Such was the case with Jim. After eight years of sales experience, he wanted to bring his business to the next level. Try as he might, however, his results were spotty. For every two steps forward, he took one step back. I asked Jim if he was willing to do an assignment that would require him to get feedback from others, and he agreed.

I began by asking him to select 3 to 5 business associates whom he trusted and knew well and whose feedback he would accept. I also asked him to select 3 to 5 personal friends who fit the same criteria. Then I asked him to write down the answers to the following questions about himself:

- What are five adjectives that describe me well?
- What are my strengths?
- What are my natural gifts and talents?
- What can I improve upon?

Finally, I asked him to ask his panel of experts to answer the same questions. Jim was happy to see how quickly they responded, and he shared their feedback with me as soon as it came in. Although many of their comments were similar to Jim's own self-assessment, two types of response astonished him. The first occurred when his panel praised him for gifts he took for granted because they came so easily to him. This included such comments as:

- Jim is especially gifted in his ability to connect with people and make them feel valued. $\sum$ Jim is very organized and an exceptional time manager. He is a great planner and sees the big picture as well as the most minute details. He is always in control in a business setting and on top of every detail.
- Jim has the ability to break complex ideas and processes down into small, understandable chunks. He also finds creative new ways to demonstrate how to do something.

The second type of response that surprised Jim had to do with the areas that needed improvement. In many cases, he was completely unaware of them! Examples included:

- In an effort to be sure he is being heard and understood, Jim sometimes makes a point more than once.
- Jim tries to filter out the important from the unimportant, but sometimes in his haste to get things done, he misses critical details.
- Jim needs to temper his efficiency with some diplomacy.
- Jim sometimes acts out a role instead of simply being who he is. This causes him to come across as untrustworthy when, in fact, he is an extremely trustworthy individual.

Although he was surprised by both types of comments, Jim took them to heart. To act on his strengths, he decided to leverage his newly-discovered ability to explain complex subjects by developing a marketing plan to deliver seminars. To address his weaknesses, he met for several coaching sessions with me. I began by asking him to prioritize the areas he wanted to work on. Then I asked him to create a specific action plan for each area.

For example, I asked Jim to write down key actions he wanted to improve upon during each sales call, such as listening to his client with empathy, slowing down the pace of his questioning process, and paying close attention to critical details. After the appointment was over, I suggested that he conduct a self-debriefing session by assessing what went well and what he would do differently next time. Jim saw positive results almost immediately. He began opening and closing more cases each week, having his calls to clients returned more promptly, and increasing his referral numbers.

Here are some additional suggestions for working with this sales success factor.

Suggestions for Working with the Accurate Self-Assessment Competency

1. Write down a list of your strengths and weaknesses in your Success Factor Development Journal. Then ask two or three friends to write down a list of your strengths and weaknesses from their point of view. Compare your list with theirs.
2. When you are interacting with people with whom you feel comfortable, ask them for feedback about your behavior. Write down their responses about your strengths and the areas where you need to improve in your Success Factor Development Journal.
3. In your Success Factor Development Journal, reflect on situations when you have felt successful/unsuccessful and analyze what was happening. Why did you feel one way or the other? Are there patterns in your behavior that lead to being successful or unsuccessful?
4. Make a video or audiotape of yourself in a client meeting or telephone call. Find someone who will watch or listen to the tape with you and offer you an analysis of your strengths weaknesses. Ask them for suggestions about how to improve your weaknesses.
5. Print and analyze your e-mails and see how people react to them. What was your intention when you wrote them and what was the result?
6. When you complete an interaction with a prospect, client or colleague, ask yourself: "How did I do?" Learn from your mistakes and celebrate your successes.

Mastery of the Sales Process

Every sales process finishes in one of two predictable ways: a successfully completed sale or a lost sale. Learning how to expertly manage the sales process will enable you to close more sales and provide the best possible care for your clients.

As you practice each of the Sales Success Factors in this cluster (Has Results Orientation, Is Adaptable, Questions and Listens Effectively, and Applies Targeted Problem Solving), your sales will close more efficiently while lost opportunities will plunge to a minimum. In addition to closing more sales with more satisfied clients, you will find the sales process more enjoyable and develop more positive relationships with your clients.

Sales Success Factor 5: Has a Results Orientation

Salespeople with a results orientation have the resolve to set challenging goals and the persistence to achieve them in the face of obstacles.

Salespeople who have a results orientation:
- Focus on measurable, challenging goals and are disciplined in following through on their action plans.
- Show a strong sense of urgency about solving problems and getting the results they desire.
- Create their own measures of excellence beyond those set by management.
- Act decisively to pursue opportunities that promise the best return on their time and effort.
- Focus on profitable sales opportunities.

Salespeople who LACK a results orientation:
- Do not take their goals seriously. They often make a token effort by setting easy or impossible goals.
- Work on a whim, without regard to past results.
- Show no standard of excellence and do only the minimum required to get by.
- Show little concern for improvement.
- Follow the path of least resistance rather than going after challenging but profitable markets and customers.
- Do not keep records or report their results to anyone.
- Resist being coached or mentored.

Exercise 1: Understanding the Results Orientation Competency

To get a better understanding of how this competency works in your life, try this exercise.

Understanding Results Orientation
Write the name of a person you know who possesses this sales success factor: ____   Describe the evidence for choosing this individual.
Write your own definition of the Results Orientation sales success factor.

Exercise 2: Applying the Results Orientation Competency

Now describe how you can use this competency to help you create a successful sales career.

How I can apply this competency in my life

Exercise 3: Practicing the Results Orientation Competency

Now that you understand more about this competency and have a clearer picture of how it might work in your sales career, it is time to practice what you have learned by creating specific affirmations for it and spending time visualizing that it is already creating success in your career.

An example of an affirmation focused on results orientation is:
- Setting challenging goals is a way of life for me.

If you scored particularly low on certain behaviors in this category of the self-assessment test, try writing an affirmation for each one. For example:
- I act decisively to pursue sales opportunities that promise the best return on my time and effort.
- It is very important to me to achieve the high sales goals I have set for myself.
- I have the tenacity to achieve my goals even in the face of obstacles.

Now write your own affirmations in the space below. Remember to keep them short and simple and to phrase them in the present tense as though you were describing your current reality. When you are done, sign your statement.

Results Orientation Affirmations

I, _______________________________ declare that the following statements are true about me:

Signed: _______________________________

Create A Daily Practice

Now that you have written and visualized your affirmations, the next step is to practice them regularly until they become second nature to you. Adhering to the following steps will greatly increase your ability to incorporate and apply the competency successfully in your life.

Set your intention, affirm and visualize. Take a few moments at the beginning and ending of each day to read through your affirmations, set your intention to incorporate them into your life, and visualize yourself easily and joyfully applying them in your sales career.

Write in your Daily Checklist and *Sales Success Factor Development Journal.* Make a few notes in the Morning/Evening section of your Daily Checklist (Appendix 2) and write down any additional thoughts that occur to you in your journal (Appendix 3).

Review your Sales Success Factors Development Plan. Be sure to create a Sales Success Factors Development Plan (Appendix 4) to help you develop this competency. Then review it daily to make sure you are on track.

Reassess, reward, revise, and repeat

After practicing your affirmations for a few weeks, reassess how you are doing on the core behaviors of this competency. If you feel that you now use all aspects of the core behaviors effectively, reward yourself. If you need more work, write a new affirmation to target the core behaviors that are still weak. Then begin the cycle again.

Case Study: Setting Goals

A study conducted by Yale University in 1956 showed that the top 3% of the graduating class had written down their goals—both short- and long-term—about what they wanted to achieve and accomplish in their lives. Thirty years later, in 1986, a follow-up study showed that this same 3% were significantly more successful than the rest of the class. The main difference was that they were still writing down their goals.

If you are serious about achieving more of the goals you set for yourself, answer the following questions.

	Questions about your goals	YES	NO
1	Are your goals written down?		
2	Are your goals written down?		
3	Are they measurable?		
4	Have you broken down your written goals into small action steps?		
5	Do you review your written goals on a daily basis?		
6	Do you modify your goals when necessary? (This includes scrapping them and replacing them when appropriate.)		
7	Do you reward yourself when you achieve a specific goal?		
8	Have you shared your goals with others who can give you valuable feedback?		
9	Have you acquired the skills, attitudes, habits and knowledge you need to attain your goals?		
10	Have you consulted with others who have already achieved the goals you seek?		

Scoring

Give yourself a score of 10 points for each Yes answer you selected.

90-100: Congratulations. You are in great shape to achieve your goals. Keep doing what you are doing.

70-89: Increase your focus on what you want to achieve and why. Set aside one hour of quiet time to review the 10 questions above and to answer the 10 questions that follow.

<70: Yes, these questions apply to you! It may be time for some introspection. Consider working with a coach.

Tracking Your Goal Progress
Ask yourself these questions at least weekly:

1. What progress am I making toward the achievement of my goal(s)?
2. What actions can I take today to move me one step closer to achieving my goal(s)?
3. What actions/activities do I need to start doing to achieve my goal(s)?
4. What actions/activities do I need to stop doing to achieve my goal(s)?
5. What actions/activities do I need to continue doing to achieve my goal(s)?
6. What obstacles do I anticipate encountering in the achievement of my goal(s)? What can I do to overcome them?
7. What support do I need from other people to achieve my goal(s)? Who can offer me such support? Have I asked them for it?
8. What additional knowledge or skills do I need to acquire to achieve my goal(s)?
9. How will I reward myself when I accomplish the key benchmarks I have set to achieve my goal(s)?
10. How will I reward myself when I fully accomplish my goal(s)?

Summary

If you are serious about wanting to achieve more in your personal or business life, consider the following advice:

The reason most people never reach their goals is that they don't define them, or ever seriously consider them as believable or achievable. Winners can tell you where they are going, what they plan to do along the way, and who will be sharing the adventure with them.
—Denis Waitley

In the absence of clearly defined goals, we become strangely loyal to performing daily trivia until ultimately we become enslaved by it.
—Robert Heinlein

Here are some additional suggestions for working with this sales success factor:

Suggestions for Working with the Results Orientation Competency

1. In your Success Factor Development Journal, evaluate your experience with goals. Have you been able to achieve both sales activity and sales results goals? If you have had trouble meeting either of these in the past, outline your strategy for meeting them in the future.
2. At the end of each day, be sure to evaluate what happened during the day. Did you achieve your goals? What worked? Why? What didn't work? Why? What could you have done differently? What assumptions do you need to challenge or change? What got in the way? How can you conquer the obstacles in yourself and in the situation the next time?
3. In your Success Factor Development Journal, keep a log of the situations where you demonstrated results orientation and of situations where you did not. Be sure to review these periodically. Another good strategy is to discuss your challenges with someone whose opinion you value and trust. Ask this person to help you assess the implications for your development.
4. Identify a sales colleague who exhibits results orientation. Ask that person how he or she stays organized and focused. Also ask your informants how they monitor their progress against goals.
5. Think about a time in your life when you were highly committed to getting something done. How did you approach the situation? How could you apply the same dedication and action to your sales career?
6. Treat performance measures as a baseline against which you track your career accomplishments, not as a target result. If you believe you have the ability to surpass performance targets, then mentally raise the bar by shooting for stretch goals over and above the target.

Sales Success Factor 6: Is Adaptable

Adaptable salespeople modify their style and approach in order to achieve a specific objective in a given situation.

Adaptable salespeople:
- Explore different possibilities rather than just the obvious ones.
- Decide what to do based on the situation.
- Are willing to change their minds in light of new evidence.
- Are able to juggle multiple demands.
- Change their plans or strategies when the initial approach does not work.

Salespeople who LACK adaptability:
- Are unable to adapt their usual sales process and tactics to changes in a customer's situation.
- Cannot handle multiple demands.
- Respond negatively to new situations, such as new pricing structures or new customer contacts.
- Display worry or emotional strain when it is necessary to shift priorities.

Exercise 1: Understanding the Adaptability Competency

To get a better understanding of how this competency works in your life, try this exercise.

<table>
<tr><td>Understanding Adaptability</td></tr>
<tr><td>Write the name of a person you know who possesses this sales success factor:

____

Describe the evidence for choosing this individual.

</td></tr>
<tr><td>Write your own definition of the Adaptability sales success factor.

</td></tr>
</table>

Exercise 2: Applying the Adaptability Competency

Now describe how you can use this competency to help you create a successful sales career.

<table>
<tr><td>How I can apply this competency in my life</td></tr>
<tr><td>

</td></tr>
</table>

Exercise 3: Practicing the Adaptability Competency

Now that you understand more about this competency and have a clearer picture of how it might work in your sales career, it is time to practice what you have learned by creating specific affirmations for it and spending time visualizing that it is already creating success in your career.

An example of an affirmation focused on adaptability is:

- I modify my style and approach in order to achieve what I am after in a given situation.

If you scored particularly low on certain behaviors in this category of the self-assessment test, try writing an affirmation for each one. For example:

- I am willing to change my mind when I see new evidence.
- I can handle several demands at the same time.
- I am flexible and can adapt when clients bring up a whole new set of facts that they have never mentioned before.

Now write your own affirmations in the space below. Remember to keep them short and simple and to phrase them in the present tense as though you were describing your current reality. When you are done, sign your statement.

Adaptability Affirmations

I, _________________________________ declare that the following statements are true about me:

Signed: _______________________________

Create A Daily Practice

Now that you have written and visualized your affirmations, the next step is to practice them regularly until they become second nature to you. Adhering to the following steps will greatly increase your ability to incorporate and apply the competency successfully in your life.

Set your intention, affirm and visualize. Take a few moments at the beginning and ending of each day to read through your affirmations, set your intention to incorporate them into your life, and visualize yourself easily and joyfully applying them in your sales career.

Write in your Daily Checklist and *Sales Success Factor Development Journal.* Make a few notes in the Morning/Evening section of your Daily Checklist (Appendix 2) and write down any additional thoughts that occur to you in your journal (Appendix 3).

Review your Sales Success Factors Development Plan. Be sure to create a Sales Success Factors Development Plan (Appendix 4) to help you develop this competency. Then review it daily to make sure you are on track.

Reassess, Reward, Revise, And Repeat

After practicing your affirmations for a few weeks, reassess how you are doing on the core behaviors of this competency. If you feel that you now use all aspects of the core behaviors effectively, reward yourself. If you need more work, write a new affirmation to target the core behaviors that are still weak. Then begin the cycle again.

Case Study: Using Data To Foster Adaptability

If you have ever heard yourself saying, "But I've always done it that way," or "That presentation isn't working the way it used to," it's time to work on the Adaptability Sales Success Factor.

Such was the case for Samantha, who was a seasoned advisor who usually produced at her company's mid-incentive club level. Her business typically resembled a roller coaster: ebbing and flowing throughout the year, but ending in a flurry of activity. This year was different. The down cycles were more prolonged, and the up cycles didn't reach their usual heights. In fact, her year ended on a prolonged down cycle.

Samantha's manager suggested that she speak with me. During our first conversation, she told me that she had been trying to upgrade her clientele and go more with a "quality vs. quantity" approach. This is a good idea in theory, but it hadn't work well for her. I discovered a number of reasons for this. One was that she did not keep good records, so she was unable to objectively look at her results to compare what was different now to when her business was going better. Another was that she never analyzed what was happening. She simply worked harder to conduct her business the way she'd always done it.

I asked Samantha to do a case-by-case analysis of the last four months of appointments. We discovered that she could, in fact, upgrade the quality of her prospects in 40% of her appointments. I then asked her to role-play with me how she obtained her appointments over the phone and how she approached her prospects during their first meeting. It soon became clear that she was using a one size fits all approach instead of flexibly adjusting her presentation to the needs of individual prospects. Her typical approach did not suit the more sophisticated prospects she aspired to work with.

Over the next few months, Samantha worked hard to turn the situation around. She came to realize that she needed more training in order to offer her higher-quality prospects more sophisticated products, so she took some advanced classes. She asked advisors who were successfully selling in this market to let her work on some joint cases so she could observe what they did and learn from them. She also worked hard to learn how to adapt her approach to the needs of individual prospects. This included changing the way she asked for appointments as well as what she said during her initial face-to-face meetings.

To alert her if her business was beginning to slide backwards again, she also agreed to put into practice an early warning system: keeping accurate activity records. This would enable her to precisely track her activity levels and effectiveness ratios, which would tell her immediately if she was performing above average or falling below par. Such data would allow her to analyze where she was off course and allow her to make timely corrections, ensuring that she would experience a great year instead of a down year.

Here are some ways you can work with your adaptability affirmations:

Suggestions for Working with the Adaptability Competency

1. In your Success Factor Development Journal, keep a log of situations where you felt you demonstrated adaptability and situations where you did not. Use the core behaviors of adaptability and review these situations for patterns.
2. Periodically review the activity management and sales processes you have in place. What are the strengths and weaknesses of each one? Is there a better, more effective way to do them?
3. The next time you are confronted with a problem in working with a prospect or client, be prepared to depart from your "traditional" approach. If there is time, speak with colleagues and brainstorm alternative approaches.
4. Be willing to make midstream adjustments when things are not going well or when situations change. When current strategies are not working, stop what you are doing, acknowledge that they are not working, and make whatever adjustments are necessary to your plans, activities, objectives and behavior.
5. Think about your usual telephone approach, fact-finding process, and sales presentation. Experiment with different styles and approaches the next few times you do these routine activities. Analyze how you felt each time and how each style was received.
6. When interacting with prospects and customers, be open to their opinions and viewpoints. Adapt your responses to their needs and be willing to accept an outcome that may be different from your initial expectation. Understanding and adapting to others' needs will greatly increase your sales effectiveness.

Sales Success Factor 7: Questions and Listens Effectively

In large part, the degree to which you are successful is contingent upon the meaningfulness and quality of the questions that you ask, as well as your ability to listen to the answers your clients and prospects give you. Developing a high level of skill in this process is not just a good idea, it is mandatory.

Sales people who are effective at questioning and listening follow a strategy that leads to a complete and mutual understanding of the problems that must be solved for prospects to get the results they desire.

Salespeople who question and listening effectively:
- Formulate a questioning strategy to help customers discover and verbalize their needs.
- Ask questions that cause customers to analyze, evaluate, speculate or express their feelings.
- Listen carefully. Whenever their customers' answers are unclear or do not contain the required information, they ask additional clarifying questions.
- Continue asking questions until all of the needed answers are given.
- Ask for reasons behind answers and evidence to support apparent conclusions.

Salespeople who LACK the ability to question and listen effectively:
- Consistently come away from fact-finding interviews not knowing what their prospect's key needs, objectives and available resources are.
- Waste time with prospects who are not qualified.
- Have trouble closing a sale because they cannot get their customers motivated enough about their needs to want to do something about them.

- Make their prospects feel like their needs are not being understood.
- Make their prospects feel like the proposed solutions do not solve their problems.

Exercise 1: Understanding the Effective Questioning and Listening Competency

To get a better understanding of how this competency works in your life, try this exercise.

Understanding Effective Questioning and Listening
Write the name of a person you know who possesses this sales success factor: ____   Describe the evidence for choosing this individual.
Write your own definition of the Effective Questioning and Listening sales success factor.

Exercise 2: Applying the Effective Questioning and Listening Competency

Now describe how you can use this competency to help you create a successful sales career.

How I can apply this competency in my life

Exercise 3: Practicing the Effective Questioning and Listening Competency

Now that you understand more about this competency and have a clearer picture of how it works in your sales career, it is time to practice what you have learned by creating specific affirmations for it and spending time visualizing that it is already creating success in your career.

An example of an affirmation focused on effective questioning and listening is:
- I am consistently able to follow a questioning strategy that leads to a complete mutual understanding of the problems that must be solved for my prospects to get the results they need from my products and services.

If you scored particularly low on certain behaviors in this category of the self-assessment test, try writing an affirmation for each one. For example:
- I am really good at asking questions that cause my customers to analyze, evaluate and express their feelings and needs.
- I listen carefully. When my prospects' answers are unclear or do not contain the information I am looking for, I ask further clarifying questions.
- When I question my prospects to determine their needs, I dig below the surface by asking them for the reasons behind their answers.

Now write your own affirmations in the space below. Remember to keep them short and simple and to phrase them in the present tense as though you were describing your current reality. When you are done, sign your statement.

Effective Questioning and Listening Affirmations

I, ______________________________ declare that the following statements are true about me:

Signed: ___________________________

Create A Daily Practice

Now that you have written and visualized your affirmations, the next step is to practice them regularly until they become second nature to you. Adhering to the following steps will greatly increase your ability to incorporate and apply the competency successfully in your life.

Set your intention, affirm and visualize. Take a few moments at the beginning and ending of each day to read through your affirmations, set your intention to incorporate them into your life, and visualize yourself easily and joyfully applying them in your sales career.

Write in your Daily Checklist and *Sales Success Factor Development Journal.* Make a few notes in the Morning/Evening section of your Daily Checklist (Appendix 2) and write down any additional thoughts that occur to you in your journal (Appendix 3).

Review your Sales Success Factors Development Plan. Be sure to create a Sales Success Factors Development Plan (Appendix 4) to help you develop this competency. Then review it daily to make sure you are on track.

Reassess, Reward, Revise, And Repeat

After practicing your affirmations for a few weeks, reassess how you are doing on the core behaviors of this competency. If you feel that you now use all aspects of the core behaviors effectively, reward yourself. If you need more work, write a new affirmation to target the core behaviors that are still weak. Then begin the cycle again.

Case Study: The Seven Factors To Becoming A Great Listener

Whether you are a salesperson, manager, boss, co-worker, parent, spouse or friend, you will need to persuade someone to do something at different times in your life. Some people believe that you need to use the spoken word to convince people to see it your way.

While the spoken word and the logic of your argument are important, effective and active listening is one of the highest forms of persuasion. Most people have a deep desire to be understood; if you are an exceptionally good listener, they will gain confidence and trust in you. When you connect with people at that level, you develop a strong relationship with them that is hard to beat.

The Seven Factors to Becoming a Great Listener

1. **Be prepared.** Before holding a face-to-face meeting or dialing the telephone, prepare yourself mentally and physically. Clear your mind of everything except the purpose of your interaction. Get comfortable, take a few deep breaths, and relax. Come prepared with thoughtful and meaningful questions that will help you understand where the other person is coming from and what his or her needs are.
2. **Don't assume anything.** Come to the interaction with an open mind. Ask open-ended questions in the spirit of genuine curiosity and desire to gain clarity. Don't treat the process like an interrogation and don't attempt to box anyone into a corner.
3. **Listen to understand.** Don't worry about what you should say next. If you do, you may hear what your prospect says, but you won't understand what he or she actually means. Paraphrase what you heard your prospect say to check your understanding and encourage further responses and clarifications. (It is often the subsequent explanations that are most revealing.)
4. **Take notes.** Ask your fellow communicator for permission to jot down some notes while he or she is speaking. This shows genuine interest in the conversation and will also help you keep your undivided attention on the speaker.
5. **Get into alignment.** One study concluded that only 7% of the meaning of an oral conversation comes from the words. Thirty-eight percent of the meaning comes from the tone of voice, while fully 55% comes from nonverbal body language cues such as facial expressions, distance between speakers, and hand and eye movements. So make sure that your words, actions, and body language are all saying the same thing.

6. **Look them in the eye.** Because eye contact shows other people that they have your undivided attention, it's virtually impossible to really hear what another person is saying unless you maintain eye contact with them. Direct eye contact keeps you focused, and it plays a huge role in nonverbal communication.

7. *Keep your cool.* Listen non-defensively and avoid being negative or argumentative. Develop a sincere curiosity and concern about others and learn how to ask open-ended questions to gain clarity.

Listening Exercise

Active listening is a skill that can be learned. To improve, you must have the desire to do so and then practice. Use these seven secrets as a checklist after each interaction with a prospect or customer.

Score yourself on each factor using a scale of 1-10, where 1 is low and 10 is high. Track your progress over time, and you will be impressed by how much you improve!

Date ________________	
The 7 Great Listener Factors	**Your Score**
1. Be prepared	
2. Don't assume anything	
3. Listen to understand	
4. Take notes	
5. Get into alignment	
6. Look them in the eye	
7. Keep your cool	

Here are some additional suggestions for working with this sales success factor.

Suggestions for Working with the Effective Questioning Competency

1. Remember that telling is not selling. If you are telling, you aren't questioning and listening, so you won't understand what is important to your customer. If you don't understand, how can you match your solution to what is important to the customer or understand what will motivate the customer to act?

2. If your organization has an approved fact-finding process with a fact-finding form and a track to go with it, practice it until you have it mastered. Then role-play the fact-finding interview with a colleague and make a video or audio recording of it. Analyze the recording in terms of the core behaviors of effective questioning and listening. In your Sales Success Factor Journal, note the core behaviors that were present and those that were absent. Describe how you can include the missing behaviors the next time you use the fact-finding process with a client.

3. As you ask questions, try to form a picture in your mind of what the customer wants. Ask questions whose answers fill in the picture for you. From time to time, share the picture with the customer to see if it is accurate.

Suggestions for Working with the Effective Questioning Competency, continued

4. No mind reading! Don't assume or guess what a person means. Ask clarifying questions to find out for real. For example, ask the client, "when you say _____, can you give me some specific examples so I can understand exactly what you mean?"
5. Get past generalities to specifics. Keep going to the next level and the next by asking a series of questions like: "How, specifically, is that a problem? If you could solve that problem, what would that allow you to do? How would that benefit your organization?"
6. Identify a colleague who is an effective questioner and listener. Ask this person to do a joint sales call with you, then carefully watch him or her ask questions. Make notes in your Success Factor Development Journal about how you can use what you have observed as a model.

Sales Success Factor 8: Applies Targeted Problem Solving

Salespeople who effectively apply targeted problem solving match priority problems in their prospects' situations with solutions that exactly meet their prospects' needs.

Salespeople who successfully apply targeted problem solving:
- Identify the cause and effect relationships in the prospect's problem situation.
- Recognize the evidence and impact of the prospect's problems.
- Peel back multiple layers of a problem to get to the core.
- Identify several possible solutions and weigh the value of each one.
- Recommend the solution(s) that will produce the best results for the prospect.

Salespeople who LACK the skill of targeted problem solving:
- Don't ask follow-up questions to delve more deeply into the causes and impacts of the problems first presented by the customer.
- Don't experiment with additional solutions beyond the obvious.
- Use the same solution to fit all client problems. When their solution doesn't fit, they lose the sale.
- Guess or assume they know what a customer's problems are rather than probing to find out.

Exercise 1: Understanding the Targeted Problem Solving Competency

To get a better understanding of how this competency works in your life, try this exercise.

Understanding Targeted Problem Solving
Write the name of a person you know who possesses this sales success factor: ____   Describe the evidence for choosing this individual.
Write your own definition of the Targeted Problem Solving sales success factor.

Exercise 2: Applying the Targeted Problem Solving Competency

Now describe how you can use this competency to help you create a successful sales career.

How I can apply this competency in my life

Exercise 3: Practicing the Targeted Problem Solving Competency

Now that you understand more about this competency and have a clearer picture of how it might work in your sales career, it is time to practice what you have learned by creating specific affirmations for it and spending time visualizing that it is already creating success in your career.

An example of an affirmation focused on targeted problem solving is:
- I am able to identify my clients' most critical problems and tailor my company's products and services to exactly meet their needs.

If you scored particularly low on certain behaviors in this category of the self-assessment test, try writing an affirmation for each one. For example:
- I am really good at helping my customers think through their situation, define their problems, and recognize the causes of those problems.
- I am able to uncover the multiple layers of the problems faced by clients and show them the most effective way to use my company's products to solve those problems.
- I tailor my recommended solutions to exactly meet my customers' needs.

Now write your own affirmations in the space below. Remember to keep them short and simple and to phrase them in the present tense as though you were describing your current reality. When you are done, sign your statement.

Targeted Problem Solving Affirmations

I, ______________________________ declare that the following statements are true about me:

Signed: ______________________________

Create a daily practice

Now that you have written and visualized your affirmations, the next step is to practice them regularly until they become second nature to you. Adhering to the following steps will greatly increase your ability to incorporate and apply the competency successfully in your life.

Set your intention, affirm and visualize. Take a few moments at the beginning and ending of each day to read through your affirmations, set your intention to incorporate them into your life, and visualize yourself easily and joyfully applying them in your sales career.

Write in your Daily Checklist and *Sales Success Factor Development Journal*. Make a few notes in the Morning/Evening section of your Daily Checklist (Appendix 2) and write down any additional thoughts that occur to you in your journal (Appendix 3).

Review your Sales Success Factors Development Plan. Be sure to create a Sales Success Factors Development Plan (Appendix 4) to help you develop this competency. Then review it daily to make sure you are on track.

Reassess, Reward, Revise, And Repeat

After practicing your affirmations for a few weeks, reassess how you are doing on the core behaviors of this competency. If you feel that you now use all aspects of the core behaviors effectively, reward yourself. If you need more work, write a new affirmation to target the core behaviors that are still weak. Then begin the cycle again.

Case Study: Pinpointing And Solving Targeted Problems

You know (or perhaps are) this type of salesperson: self-assured, self-confident, and always ready to offer advice and counsel to prospects and clients.

Kevin fit this description perfectly. He just had one small problem: transitioning from a meeting with his prospects to asking for—and getting—an order! Most salespeople have a 33% closing ratio (one successful closing appointment for every three attempts), but Kevin's was 20% (one successful closing for every five attempts). This made the difference between success and failure.

Kevin was desperate to understand why his closing ratio was so low. I soon discovered several major challenges that revolved around his communication skills and overall professionalism. For example, due to an "in your face" style, Kevin struggled to break the ice and make a good first impression. His prospects (and even some of his clients) viewed him as a typical salesperson who only wanted to sell them something instead of as a consultant who had their best interests at heart.

Kevin also failed to understand a key issue: each of us has a unique style of communication and unconsciously seeks to be approached in a style that closely matches our own. For example, some people are unable to express their needs and wants to a salesperson until they have developed a relationship with them. They need to establish areas of common ground—perhaps by talking about family, jobs, hobbies, or even the weather—before getting down to business. Other people are completely put off by such "chit chat" and want to get down to business right away.

Kevin was an expert at communicating with the no chit chat group, but he needed help building rapport with the relationship group. We began by creating some strategies he could use to put people at ease. I suggested that he prepare for his appointments by taking a moment to put himself in his prospects' place. What kind of body language would make them feel comfortable? Uncomfortable? How quickly should he speak? What tone of voice should he use? What kind of questions should he ask or comments should he make that would develop rapport?

Then we began to work on Kevin's fact-finding and listening skills. His typical approach to the interview step of the sales process was to pepper his prospects with rapid-fire questions. After all (he thought), he just needed information to put a proposal together—even though his proposals looked alarmingly alike. This made most of his prospects question whether he was sincerely trying to solve *their* problems. As a result, they offered less and less information in response to his questions.

In fact, Kevin did not understand the basic human principle that Ron Willingham expresses so well in his book *Integrity Selling for the 21st Century:*

People are more apt to trust and open up to you when you listen to them, care about them, and have a sincere desire to understand them

.

Once we had discussed this principle, Kevin made great strides in his ability to apply it. His empathy for his prospects and clients grew, and he learned how to carefully paraphrase what they said to make sure he had understood them correctly. He discovered that this process often led his prospects to open up to him and explain more thoroughly what they meant or the reasoning behind their answers.

Kevin needed to improve one final area of the Targeted Problem Solving Sales Success Factor. Quite simply, he needed to become more of a professional. His knowledge of his industry was limited; while this was good enough for a small number of prospects, it prevented him from being fully aware of the depth and breadth of the problems his clients and prospects faced and how he could solve them.

I suggested that he become a student of his business by following the philosophy of life-long learning. He agreed to do so and enrolled in an industry designation course of study, setting up a schedule that enabled him to obtain his first industry designation in 24 months. He also began to attend his company's training programs in earnest and to avail himself of the wealth of support material his company provided.

Today Kevin's closing ratio has improved greatly. He continues to conduct a self-debriefing after each appointment to assess what went well and what he will do differently next time. And his increasing levels of knowledge have not only enabled him to recognize and solve more of his clients' problems, but to upgrade them as well. The result has been more sophisticated sales, larger cases, and a dramatic increase in referrals from happy clients.

Here are some additional suggestions for working with this sales success factor:

Suggestions for Working with the Targeted Problem Solving Competency

1. Once you discover a problem or potential problem when getting the facts about a prospect's situation, go deeper. Develop a mutual understanding of the factors causing the problem so that you can consider and address each of these factors in your recommended solutions.
2. Get together with a group of colleagues and brainstorm solutions to particularly troublesome problems that you have all run into with past customers. In your Success Factor Development Journal, list the problems you discuss and the different solutions the group comes up with.
3. Be alert to the times when you successfully target problem solving to understand and meet a customer's needs. When this happens, give yourself credit for it and make some notes in your Success Factor Development Journal describing what you did. This will help you repeat your targeted problem solving success with your next customer.
4. Get in the habit of generating several solutions to each client's problems. Explore the trade-offs of costs and benefits with the client. Help them evaluate the long- and short-range advantages of each alternative. Present the solution you think is best, but have the others available as a backup if you need them.
5. Study the options available within your company's product lines and make notes in your Success Factor Development Journal about the best situations in which to use them with a client.

Mastery of Customer Relationships

How others perceive you proves critical to the success of every insurance salesperson. Potential clients judge you and your company based on how they perceive your motivation. When clients feel that you genuinely have their best interests in mind, they are likely to invest in you and your company. Developing the Sales Success Factors in this cluster (Focuses on Customer Success, Has Interpersonal Sensitivity, and Gains Commitment) helps you communicate genuine concern for your clients.

Sales Success Factor 9: Focuses on Customer Success

Salespeople who effectively focus on customer success constantly seek to understand and respond to their customers' needs.

Salespeople who focus on customer success:
- Invest time and energy to understand the customer's entire situation by immersing themselves in the customer's goals, needs and problems.
- Help their customers clarify and prioritize their needs and expectations.
- Focus on helping their customers succeed.
- Act as their customer's advocate within the company.
- Help their customers think through how a proposed solution can best meet their needs.

Salespeople who LACK a focus on customer success:
- Put themselves in an adversarial relationship with their customers and simply push their company's products instead of taking the time to truly understand and meet their customers' needs.
- Don't stay in touch with the customer once the sale is closed.
- Let customers fend for themselves with the company after the sale rather than acting as an intermediary to ensure the customer is satisfied.
- Make the sale rather than an ally. As a result, they fail to get referrals from their customers.

Exercise 1: Understanding the Focus on Customer Success Competency

To get a better understanding of how this competency works in your life, try this exercise.

<table>
<tr><td>Understanding Focus on Customer Success</td></tr>
<tr><td>Write the name of a person you know who possesses this sales success factor:

____

Describe the evidence for choosing this individual.

</td></tr>
<tr><td>Write your own definition of the Focus on Customer Success sales success factor.

</td></tr>
</table>

Exercise 2: Applying the Focus on Customer Success Competency

Now describe how you can use this competency to help you create a successful sales career.

<table>
<tr><td>How I can apply this competency in my life</td></tr>
<tr><td>

</td></tr>
</table>

Exercise 3: Practicing the Focus on Customer Success Competency

Now that you understand more about this competency and have a clearer picture of how it might work in your sales career, it is time to practice what you have learned by creating specific affirmations for it and spending time visualizing that it is already creating success in your career.

An example of an affirmation focused on customer success is:
- I strive to understand and exactly meet my customers' needs.

If you scored particularly low on certain behaviors in this category of the self-assessment test, try writing an affirmation for each one. For example:
- I act as an advocate to be sure my customers get the best possible service from my company.
- My primary intent is helping my clients succeed by recommending solutions that exactly meet their needs.
- I make sure my customers understand how to get the maximum benefit from the solutions I recommend.

Now write your own affirmations in the space below. Remember to keep them short and simple and to phrase them in the present tense as though you were describing your current reality. When you are done, sign your statement.

Focus on Customer Success Affirmations

I, _______________________________ declare that the following statements are true about me:

Signed: _______________________________

Create A Daily Practice

Now that you have written and visualized your affirmations, the next step is to practice them regularly until they become second nature to you. Adhering to the following steps will greatly increase your ability to incorporate and apply the competency successfully in your life.

Set your intention, affirm and visualize. Take a few moments at the beginning and ending of each day to read through your affirmations, set your intention to incorporate them into your life, and visualize yourself easily and joyfully applying them in your sales career.

Write in your Daily Checklist and *Sales Success Factor Development Journal*. Make a few notes in the Morning/Evening section of your Daily Checklist (Appendix 2) and write down any additional thoughts that occur to you in your journal (Appendix 3).

Review your Sales Success Factors Development Plan. Be sure to create a Sales Success Factors Development Plan (Appendix 4) to help you develop this competency. Then review it daily to make sure you are on track.

Reassess, Reward, Revise, And Repeat

After practicing your affirmations for a few weeks, reassess how you are doing on the core behaviors of this competency. If you feel that you now use all aspects of the core behaviors effectively, reward yourself. If you need more work, write a new affirmation to target the core behaviors that are still weak. Then begin the cycle again.

Case Study: Focusing On Client Success

In addition to coaching advisors one-on-one, I also conduct *Champions' Success Groups©*. These consist of eight to twelve sales associates who all have the same goal in mind: solving practice management problems and increasing sales. It was during one of these calls that the following problem surfaced.

Sam told the group that he took great pride in offering his prospects and clients the best, most appropriate solutions to their problems that he could. He said he was absolutely committed to helping them achieve their stated goals and objectives, which he uncovered during a fact finding interview. So what was his problem? Sam said he often ended up arguing with his prospect about the best solution. In spite of this, however, he proudly added, "In nine out of ten cases I make the sale."

After this assertion, a group member asked, "What kind of ongoing relationship do you have with your clients and how many referrals do you receive from them?" There was a long pause on the line. Finally, Sam replied that he made fewer multiple product sales to the same clients than others in his office and that he rarely even asked for—let alone received—any referrals.

This spurred more questions from the group and led to a general discussion about best practices. The consensus was that Sam was more interested in making the sale than in serving his clients' long-term needs. Sam admitted that he only asked enough questions to put together a proposal. It wasn't that what he proposed was wrong (hence his strong closing ratio), but that he didn't invest the time and energy necessary to fully understand his customers' dreams, goals, and challenges.

The group also observed that Sam was a generalist whose knowledge of his market only skimmed the surface. As a result, we advised him to study his market's needs and challenges in depth. Once he had done so, we advised him to target a niche market. First, however, he needed to broaden his overall knowledge.

I recommended that he contact several current clients with whom he had a good relationship and ask them probing questions about their unique problems and issues. For example: "What really matters to you? What keeps you up at night? What publications do you read? What conventions and trade shows do you attend? If you could solve just one problem in your business, what would it be?"

In addition, I suggested that the next time he attended a company training program or seminar, he should listen actively for ideas that could benefit his clients and prospects. "As soon as you hear something," I said, "jot it down. Then, at the next break, call your client and say something like 'John, this is Sam. I'm calling you from an advanced seminar I'm attending, and I came across a great idea that could benefit you and your company. I'd like to stop by next week to share it with you. Would Tuesday morning or Thursday afternoon be more convenient for you?'"

Another group member suggested that Sam become an article clipper. "Whenever you see an article that could benefit a client or prospect, cut it out and send it to them with a brief note."

Sam didn't bring the subject up again for two months. When he did, he admitted that he had been reluctant at first to implement any of the changes the group had suggested. In fact, he had completely dismissed them. Then, while attending a seminar one day, something just clicked. He heard an idea that would greatly benefit one of his prospects, so he called him up and asked for an appointment. The meeting lasted two hours. At the end of the meeting, the prospect told Sam that he greatly appreciated the ideas that Sam had shared with him. This led to a proposal that included multiple purchases. When Sam delivered the policy, he asked for referrals and received several.

Sam said that he now intended to follow through with all of our suggestions. He also said that he finally understood why focusing his attention on helping his prospects and clients succeed was so much more powerful than simply trying to make the sale.

Here are some additional suggestions for working with this sales success factor:

Suggestions for Working with the Focus on Customer Success Competency

1. Believe in the value of your service to your prospects. See yourself as a sales professional who has the commitment, skills, products and services your prospects need to exactly meet their needs.
2. Study the options available within your company's product lines. Think about how you could use your skills and product lines to help each of your prospects find the solution that is right for them. Make notes about this in your Success Factor Development Journal.
3. Identify salespeople in your organization who demonstrate the focus on customer success competency. Ask them how they determine how particular clients can best use specific company products and services. Ask them to take you out on a sales call with them so you can observe how they do it. Use what you learn as a "focus on customer success" model. Make notes about all of this in your Success Factor Development Journal.
4. Be alert to the times when you are particularly effective at focusing on your customer's success. When this happens, give yourself credit for it, feel good about it, and note down the circumstances in your Success Factor Development Journal. This will help you apply this process to your next customer.
5. Stay in touch with your customers after the sale and act on their behalf with your company. Make certain that all goes well with the delivery, installation, and service provided by your company. Teach your customers how to get the best, most successful use out of the products they purchase from you.

Sales Success Factor 10: Has Interpersonal Sensitivity

Salespeople who are high in interpersonal sensitivity recognize and respond to the feelings, attitudes and motivations of others.

Salespeople who have interpersonal sensitivity:
- Have the ability to see things from another's perspective.
- Acknowledge the unique experiences, backgrounds and perspectives of others.
- Notice and adjust their own actions in response to others' verbal and non-verbal behavior (e.g., body language, tone of voice, innuendo).
- Understand where another person's feelings are coming from and respond appropriately.
- Recognize the concerns and interests of others.

Salespeople who LACK interpersonal sensitivity:
- Tend to drive sales interviews in terms of their own feelings, not those of their customers.
- Are unable to read people well and often misunderstand what they are thinking and feeling.
- Are often surprised by the feelings and actions of others.
- Appear to be indifferent or uncaring, which makes their prospects and customers less willing to communicate with them.

Exercise 1: Understanding the Interpersonal Sensitivity Competency

To get a better understanding of how this competency works in your life, try this exercise.

Understanding Interpersonal Sensitivity

Write the name of a person you know who possesses this sales success factor:

____

Describe the evidence for choosing this individual.

Write your own definition of the Interpersonal Sensitivity sales success factor.

Exercise 2: Applying the Interpersonal Sensitivity Competency

Now describe how you can use this competency to help you create a successful sales career.

How I can apply this competency in my life

Exercise 3: Practicing the Interpersonal Sensitivity Competency

Now that you understand more about this competency and have a clearer picture of how it might work in your sales career, it is time to practice what you have learned by creating specific affirmations for it and spending time visualizing that it is already creating success in your career.

An example of an affirmation focused on interpersonal sensitivity is:
- I am really good at recognizing and responding to the feelings, attitudes and motivations of others.

If you scored particularly low on certain behaviors in this category of the self-assessment test, try writing an affirmation for each one. For example:
- When working with others I am able to see things from their perspective.
- I am aware that not everyone sees things the same way I do; everyone has their own background and past experiences, which influence their perspective.
- I understand and respect where other peoples' feelings are coming from. This allows me to respond appropriately to them.

Now write your own affirmations in the space below. Remember to keep them short and simple and to phrase them in the present tense as though you were describing your current reality. When you are done, sign your statement.

<table>
<tr><td>Interpersonal Sensitivity Affirmations</td></tr>
<tr><td>I, _________________________________ declare that the following statements are true about me:

Signed: _____________________________</td></tr>
</table>

Create A Daily Practice

Now that you have written and visualized your affirmations, the next step is to practice them regularly until they become second nature to you. Adhering to the following steps will greatly increase your ability to incorporate and apply the competency successfully in your life.

> **Set your intention, affirm and visualize.** Take a few moments at the beginning and ending of each day to read through your affirmations, set your intention to incorporate them into your life, and visualize yourself easily and joyfully applying them in your sales career.

> **Write in your Daily Checklist and *Sales Success Factor Development Journal.*** Make a few notes in the Morning/Evening section of your Daily Checklist (Appendix 2) and write down any additional thoughts that occur to you in your journal (Appendix 3).

> **Review your Sales Success Factors Development Plan.** Be sure to create a Sales Success Factors Development Plan (Appendix 4) to help you develop this competency. Then review it daily to make sure you are on track.

Reassess, Reward, Revise, And Repeat

After practicing your affirmations for a few weeks, reassess how you are doing on the core behaviors of this competency. If you feel that you now use all aspects of the core behaviors effectively, reward yourself. If you need more work, write a new affirmation to target the core behaviors that are still weak. Then begin the cycle again.

Case Study: Putting Yourself In Your Prospect's Shoes

It is a luxury to be understood.
—Ralph Waldo Emerson

 Each of us views the world through our own filters and assigns our personal val ues to different situations. For example, some parents feel that their children should help pay for college, while others feel it is their responsibility to pay 100% of college expenses. Which view is correct? The answer is neither, of course. Both positions can be easily justified, so arguing over which one is correct is an exercise in futility and frustration.

People naturally bring their different values and styles of communication into the sales process, too. The most successful sales people understand this and develop the ability to adjust their presentations to the needs of the person with whom they are communicating. They understand that the most important factor for their prospects is that the sales person understand their problems, desires, goals, and expectations—not just try to sell them something.

I was reminded of this fact when Dan, an advisor with 2 1/2 years of experience, contacted me and asked, "Why do I always get the same objections over and over again? What am I doing wrong?"

Dan explained that about 25% of his prospects appreciated his ideas and quickly bought his solutions. But the majority did not. Instead, they raised one objection after another—most of which caught Dan by surprise. As a result, he was starting to dread his regular meetings with his manager because his assessments of pending cases were always over-optimistic and frequently just plain wrong.

I asked Dan to demonstrate his sales presentation to me and discovered that he practically raced through the process. As a result, it was easy to understand why only those clients who shared the value of speed and brevity responded positively to him. The feeling he gave most people, however, was that he didn't really care about them or understand their issues. "It's not about you, it's about them," I explained.

To help Dan increase sensitivity to his prospects' values and styles of communication, I suggested that he experiment with the following strategy.

Visualization and Implementation Strategy

Shortly before an appointment with a client or customer, go to a place where you will be undisturbed for a few minutes. Close your eyes, take a few deep breaths, and visualize yourself in your prospect's shoes. In other words, pretend that you are your prospect and that another person is asking you a question about your key needs. Then listen carefully to the reply that "you" give.

Try to keep an open mind during this process. Simply listen for answers without prejudging or negating anything that you hear. Now open your eyes and write down on a piece of paper what "you" said your key needs were. Finally, write down several open-ended questions (those that begin with words like "why, how, what, where, when, who, and where") focused on these key needs.

Practice your presentation before the appointment and record yourself in order to self-critique your delivery. Have someone you trust evaluate your presentation for overall effectiveness and how you come across. Often this simple tool of evaluation will dramatically improve the way your client perceives you. In addition you will see a marked improvement in your closing ratios.

Then go to the appointment with your prospect. During your meeting, ask the open-ended questions you created after your visualization. Don't stop with the first answer that your prospect gives you, however. Ask enough follow-up questions to acquire a deep understanding of the prospect and the issue. Be sure to listen carefully to your prospect's answers while giving them 100% of your attention. In other words, don't start thinking about your answer while your prospect is talking. Jot down your prospect's key points on a piece of paper; before you respond to them, pause and give yourself enough time to gather your thoughts. Paraphrase what your prospect said to be sure you understood them correctly, and then respond.

Also take note of your prospect's body language and non-verbal cues. Did they seem comfortable or uncomfortable when they answered a particular question? Respond in an animated tone of voice or in a monotone? Seem interested or disinterested in any given topic?

After the meeting ends, take a few minutes to review what happened. Write down what went well, what you will do differently next time, and how close your visualization came to identifying your prospect's key needs. Finally, summarize what you learned from this process in your *Sales Success Factor Development Journal.*

Dan's Results

At first Dan complained that this technique would be hard to remember and require too much work. I told him that learning any new behavior was uncomfortable at first but becomes second nature with practice. Dan agreed to experiment with the technique and soon reported that it was working really well for him. He said meetings had become more like conversations than sales calls, and that objections and surprises had diminished to nearly zero.

When your prospects and clients believe that you truly understand them, they will open up to you and treat you like a trusted advisor, not like someone who is trying to sell them something.

Here are some ways you can work with your interpersonal sensitivity affirmations:

Suggestions for Working with the Interpersonal Sensitivity Competency

1. In your Success Factor Development Journal, keep a log of situations in which you feel you demonstrated interpersonal sensitivity and situations in which you did not. Pay particular attention to critical incidents that provided opportunities for you to:
   - Identify underlying concerns and interests not explicitly expressed by your prospects and clients.
   - Adjust your actions in response to your customers' verbal or non-verbal behavior.
2. Select three people in your life whom you intensely dislike and three whom you love and admire. Write down what it is you like/dislike about them. Your goal is to unravel your gut feelings about them and to understand why your feelings are the way they are. What does this tell you about yourself? About your values and expectations?

> **Suggestions for Working with the Interpersonal Sensitivity Competency, continued**
>
> 3. Make a habit of paying attention to your gut reactions. Try to understand why you like or dislike someone and keep track of these insights in your Success Factor Development Journal.
> 4. Pay attention to the nonverbal behavior of others. When listening to your clients, don't just pay attention to their words, but also to their nonverbal messages. Pay particular attention to their facial expressions and try to determine the feelings behind their words. Make note of concerns or issues that you sense, but that are not verbalized.
> 5. Identify people in your organization whose perceptions and awareness of customers you admire. Have a discussion with them about how they developed such a good understanding of other people. Use what you learn to develop your own insights.
> 6. Try to develop ease and skill in helping other people articulate their feelings, especially their strong feelings.
> 7. Determine a set number of times each month (say 10), when you will review at the end of the day whether you showed appropriate interpersonal sensitivity to your prospects, clients and coworkers.
>   - Did you take time to listen when someone expressed his or her feelings to you? Or did you just move ahead with your own agenda?
>   - Did you practice using open-ended questions such as "Tell me more about that"?
>   - Did you fully understand both the emotions and the content behind their words?
>   - Did you adjust your style and approach to the needs and style of the person with whom you were talking? For example, were you aware of—and did you match— their body language (gestures and facial expressions)? Their verbal expressions (tone, pitch, speed, volume of the voice)? Their use of space? Their style of address (formal or casual)?
>   - Did you understand the underlying motivations for your customers' behavior? For example, did you recognize that they come from different backgrounds than you do? Have different values and beliefs? Did you adjust your responses accordingly?
> 8. If you discover that your interpersonal sensitivity skills are inadequate, determine to improve your performance. Carefully think through what the obstacles might be. For example, are you so focused on your own goals that taking time to listen to others' problems seems like an irrelevant distraction from getting important things done?

Sales Success Factor 11: Gains Commitment

Sales people who excel at gaining commitment have the ability to convince others of the worthiness of an idea or course of action, obtain their support, and get them to act accordingly.

Salespeople who excel at gaining commitment:
- Create and take advantage of opportunities to gain credibility.
- Have the ability to calculate the rational and emotional impacts of their own actions or words on others.
- Attract the attention of others and communicate with them in ways they want to hear.
- Present logical, fact-based data that motivates others to take action.
- Can demonstrate to others that a proposed action will solve their problems and have the positive impact they desire.

Salespeople who LACK the skill of gaining commitment:
- Are unable to defend a good idea if they are challenged.
- Are unable to help prospects see the advantages of using their company's products and services.
- Fail to close sales.
- Have a hard time inspiring confidence in others and being taken seriously.

Exercise 1: Understanding the Gaining Commitment Competency

To get a better understanding of how this competency works in your life, try this exercise.

Understanding Gaining Commitment
Write the name of a person you know who possesses this sales success factor: ____ Describe the evidence for choosing this individual.
Write your own definition of the Gaining Commitment sales success factor.

Exercise 2: Applying the Gaining Commitment Competency

Now describe how you can use this competency to help you create a successful sales career.

How I can apply this competency in my life

Exercise 3: Practicing the Gaining Commitment Competency

Now that you understand more about this competency and have a clearer picture of how it might work in your sales career, it is time to practice what you have learned by creating specific affirmations for it and spending time visualizing that it is already creating success in your career.

An example of an affirmation focused on gaining commitment is:
- One of my strengths as a sales person is my ability to convince others of the rightness of an idea or course of action, thereby gaining their support and getting them to act accordingly.

If you scored particularly low on certain behaviors in this category of the self-assessment test, try writing an affirmation for each one. For example:
- I am able to get people's attention and communicate with them in a way they want to hear.
- I think about the impact of what I say and do on others.
- I present logical, fact-based data to motivate others to action.

Now write your own affirmations in the space below. Remember to keep them short and simple and to phrase them in the present tense as though you were describing your current reality. When you are done, sign your statement.

Gaining Commitment Affirmations

I, ________________________________ declare that the following statements are true about me:

Signed: ________________________________

Create A Daily Practice

Now that you have written and visualized your affirmations, the next step is to practice them regularly until they become second nature to you. Adhering to the following steps will greatly increase your ability to incorporate and apply the competency successfully in your life.

Set your intention, affirm and visualize. Take a few moments at the beginning and ending of each day to read through your affirmations, set your intention to incorporate them into your life, and visualize yourself easily and joyfully applying them in your sales career.

Write in your Daily Checklist and *Sales Success Factor Development Journal*. Make a few notes in the Morning/Evening section of your Daily Checklist (Appendix 2) and write down any additional thoughts that occur to you in your journal (Appendix 3).

Review your Sales Success Factors Development Plan. Be sure to create a Sales Success Factors Development Plan (Appendix 4) to help you develop this competency. Then review it daily to make sure you are on track.

Reassess, Reward, Revise, And Repeat

After practicing your affirmations for a few weeks, reassess how you are doing on the core behaviors of this competency. If you feel that you now use all aspects of the core behaviors effectively, reward yourself. If you need more work, write a new affirmation to target the core behaviors that are still weak. Then begin the cycle again.

Case Study: The Pre-Conditions For Gaining Commitment

Seek First to Understand, then to be Understood.
—Stephen Covey

There's an old adage that says adults never argue with their own data. Another one is that people like to buy, but they hate to be sold. What does this have to do with making sales and gaining commitment? Marilyn, an advisor with four years of sales experience, could explain it to you very well.

Before entering the financial services industry, Marilyn managed the employee benefits division within the human resources department of a large company. Her staff of six thought very highly of her because she was an excellent manager and created a positive environment in which to work. In turn, she was accustomed to giving directions and having them carried out. After her company went through a merger and downsizing, Marilyn became unhappy with her job. Wanting more control over her own destiny, she accepted a commission sales position focused on employee benefits. It was a natural fit, so her product learning curve was not as steep as it is for most people who enter the business. Yet success eluded her. Marilyn told me that she was excellent at gathering facts and putting together elaborate proposals for her prospects, who assured her that they appreciated all her hard work. She was confident that her solutions were in the best interest of her prospects, and she thought they agreed with her recommendations. It was only when she asked them to sign the application that she discovered they did not.

To assess the situation, I asked Marilyn several questions:
- Do you frequently experience unforeseen objections that seem to pop up from left field?
- During your fact-finding interview, what percentage of time do you spend talking to your prospects? What percentage of time do you spend listening to them?
- When your prospects raise objections, do you welcome them, or do you feel like you need to defend your position?
- Do your prospects express a need before you recommend a solution?
- Do you clearly demonstrate how specific features of your solution address your prospects' unique needs? Or do you merely highlight the general features of your solution?
- Do you take the time to re-establish a relationship with your prospects before you move forward with the presentation of your solution?
- Do you ask trial closing questions that call for your prospects' opinions before you ask them for a final decision?

As you may have guessed, Marilyn admitted that she did most of the talking and reacted defensively to objections. The more she tried to change her prospects' thinking, the more they resisted her solutions. In *Integrity Selling for the 21st Century*, Ron Willingham says that three conditions must be met before it is possible to move forward successfully with the sales process:

1. The prospect must express a need.
2. The prospect must express a desire to do something about this need.
3. The prospect must admit they have a desire to do something about this need with you.

Unless all three conditions have been met, it will be difficult to close the sale successfully. After I introduced this concept to Marilyn, she began to understand that she had failed to establish these conditions. I further explained that this can be the result of a failure to:

- Completely understand your prospects' needs and desires.
- Listen to what your prospects mean by what they say.
- Develop rapport and a trusting, win-win relationship.
- Adequately link your solution to your prospects' goals and problems.
- Identify and speak with the real decision maker.
- Ask trial closing questions.

To gain commitment, I told her, you need to develop a sales process that you follow nearly 100% of the time on every sales call you make. Almost all of your time and effort should be focused on developing a positive, trusting relationship with your prospect; asking for the order should be the easiest and shortest part of this process. To do this, I explained, you must understand your prospect's needs as clearly as you can and then link your solutions to each one. Your goal is to ensure that both you and your prospect feel like the process will end in a win-win situation.

I also told Marilyn that she needed to be certain her prospects were tracking with her throughout the presentation, that they clearly understood how the process was benefiting them. To ascertain this, I suggested that she frequently ask her prospects to share their opinions and then listen carefully to their answers. Such a step, I said, would demonstrate her respect for her prospects, give her valuable insight into their thinking, help her anticipate their concerns (read objections), and give her the information she needs to respond effectively.

To do this, I suggested that Marilyn ask such questions as:

- Do you have any questions at this point that I could answer?
- Does this idea address your concerns?
- Have I presented anything at this point that needs more explanation?
- Is there anything else we need to talk about or explore?

Finally, I suggested that Marilyn change her overall paradigm and subsequent behavior with prospects. Instead of treating them like equals, she was treating them like employees to whom she could give orders, and it just wasn't working. I also told her that anytime a salesperson is more interested in winning an argument than in understanding the prospects' concerns, the sale is at risk.

Our discussion was a pivotal moment for her. To begin the change process, she took some index cards and wrote down on them the descriptions of the new behaviors she wanted to acquire. She reviewed the cards before every appointment and critiqued herself after each appointment, noting what she did well and what she still needed to improve. She also prepared open-ended and trial closing questions in advance. The outcome was that her closing rate improved greatly.

Here are some additional suggestions for working with this sales success factor:

Suggestions for Working with the Gaining Commitment Competency

1. In your Success Factor Development Journal, keep a log of situations in which you feel you have demonstrated the ability to gain commitment and situations in which you did not. Discuss these examples with another person and ask him or her to help you assess the implications for your development.
2. Form a study group with your colleagues. Together, draw upon each others' successful experiences in gaining commitment and reality-test future strategies. Debrief your experiences about how you presented solutions to customers and closed the sale. What worked? What would be more effective next time? Make notes in your Success Factor Development Journal on the ideas coming from the group.
3. Before attempting to gain customers' commitments, try to anticipate how they might react by determining their key issues. Use this insight to shape your presentation.
4. Recall a time when you saw someone take a dramatic action to influence a situation. How can you apply this strategy to ensure greater impact in your next closing interview?
5. As you work with customers, try to determine what their strongest values are and communicate with them in similar terms. For example, if they value facts, principles, logic and consistency, emphasize practical facts, figures and statistics in your proposal. If they value emotions and relationships, emphasize the human aspect in your proposal, showing how it will impact people and relationships in their lives. If they have an overriding vision for the future, listen carefully to their dreams and focus your proposal on how it will help them turn their vision into reality. If they value being in charge and know exactly what they want, make sure your proposal is tight, efficient, and clearly meets their objectives. Also give them options from which to choose.
6. Identify and observe others who seem to have an engaging way of communicating and gaining credibility. Pay particular attention to their non-verbal behavior. What are they doing? What visual aids do they use to help them get their message across?

Chapter 8   Mastery of Own Business

Are you an expert at managing yourself, the sales process, and customer relationships? If so, what more do you need? Ultimately, your ability to build your business will dictate your success or failure. The Sales Success Factors in this cluster include: Has Entrepreneurial Drive, Uses Key Information Effectively, Increases Customer Value, and Builds a Team. With a little practice and direction, anyone can develop and refine these behaviors to build a dynamic sales practice.

Sales Success Factor 12: Has Entrepreneurial Drive

Sales people with a high entrepreneurial drive are committed to the development of business opportunities and determined to overcome obstacles on the path to success.

Salespeople who have entrepreneurial drive:
- Take pride in being a sales professional with a sense of vision and mission about the work.
- Thrive on challenge and seek out opportunities that require some risk-taking and inventiveness to achieve a worthwhile goal.
- Focus their energy on continuous personal improvement.
- Take initiative in finding creative solutions to their clients' needs and new ways of doing business.

Salespeople who LACK entrepreneurial drive:
- Show no commitment to their sales career and do the bare minimum to get by.
- Do just the mechanics of the job—without enthusiasm or passion for becoming more and more effective.
- Need to have goals set for them and cannot work independently to an internal standard.
- Stay in the same rut of doing the same old things in the same old way.
- Fail to pursue new markets and greater levels of client service.

Exercise 1: Understanding the Entrepreneurial Drive Competency

To get a better understanding of how this competency works in your life, try this exercise.

<table>
<tr><td>Understanding Entrepreneurial Drive</td></tr>
<tr><td>Write the name of a person you know who possesses this sales success factor:

____

Describe the evidence for choosing this individual.

</td></tr>
<tr><td>Write your own definition of the Entrepreneurial Drive sales success factor.

</td></tr>
</table>

Exercise 2: Applying the Entrepreneurial Drive Competency

Now describe how you can use this competency to help you create a successful sales career.

<table>
<tr><td>How I can apply this competency in my life</td></tr>
<tr><td>

</td></tr>
</table>

Exercise 3: Practicing the Entrepreneurial Drive Competency

Now that you understand more about this competency and have a clearer picture of how it might work in your sales career, it is time to practice what you have learned by creating specific affirmations for it and spending time visualizing that it is already creating success in your career.

An example of an affirmation focused on entrepreneurial drive is:
- I have the drive to develop business opportunities and the determination to overcome obstacles on my path to success.

If you scored particularly low on certain behaviors in this category of the self-assessment test, try writing an affirmation for each one. For example:
- I take pride in being a sales professional with a sense of mission about my work.
- Day after day, I focus my energy on continuous personal improvement.
- I continue to pursue new markets.
- I provide greater and greater levels of client service.

Now write your own affirmations in the space below. Remember to keep them short and simple and to phrase them in the present tense as though you were describing your current reality. When you are done, sign your statement.

Entrepreneurial Drive Affirmations

I, _______________________________ declare that the following statements are true about me:

Signed: _______________________________

Entrepreneurs recognize opportunities and act decisively to take advantage of them. Look back over the past year. If you missed any opportunities in your business or personal life, use the following exercise to analyze the causes and develop some new resolutions and skills.

Exercise 4: Responding to Opportunities Plan

In your Success Factor Development Journal, draw a vertical line down the center of a page. In the left column, list the opportunities that came your way over the past year. Begin with your job, then move on to opportunities in your personal life. In the right column, jot down how you responded to each opportunity. Did you take full advantage of the opportunity or miss it altogether? Did you respond enthusiastically or half-heartedly to it?

Note the reasons for your responses and the outcomes. Look for patterns in your successes and failures to gain advantage from your opportunities. Finally, develop a responding to opportunities improvement plan. Ask your colleagues, family and friends to review your plan and help you implement it.

Create A Daily Practice

Now that you have written and visualized your affirmations, the next step is to practice them regularly until they become second nature to you. Adhering to the following steps will greatly increase your ability to incorporate and apply the competency successfully in your life.

Set your intention, affirm and visualize. Take a few moments at the beginning and ending of each day to read through your affirmations, set your intention to incorporate them into your life, and visualize yourself easily and joyfully applying them in your sales career.

Write in your Daily Checklist and *Sales Success Factor Development Journal*. Make a few notes in the Morning/Evening section of your Daily Checklist (Appendix 2) and write down any additional thoughts that occur to you in your journal (Appendix 3).

Review your Sales Success Factors Development Plan. Be sure to create a Sales Success Factors Development Plan (Appendix 4) to help you develop this competency. Then review it daily to make sure you are on track.

Reassess, Reward, Revise, And Repeat

After practicing your affirmations for a few weeks, reassess how you are doing on the core behaviors of this competency. If you feel that you now use all aspects of the core behaviors effectively, reward yourself. If you need more work, write a new affirmation to target the core behaviors that are still weak. Then begin the cycle again.

Case Study: Entrepreneurial Drive Can Be Developed

Stan worked as an employee in his company's home office for fifteen years. Due to his expertise, he often went into the field to help sales executives present proposals to prospects. The people who worked with him—both inside and outside the home office—regarded him highly and said he was often responsible for bringing the sale over the finish line.

Unfortunately, management eliminated Stan's department. Instead of letting him go, however, they offered him the opportunity to become an independent sales executive himself. They agreed to pay his salary for six months while he was building his business and to allow him to continue going out on calls with other sales executives on a commission split basis. Although the transition went well initially, Stan failed to take the initiative to build his own business. Instead, he simply sat back and waited for sales executives to call him for help on a joint case.

Sales people who possess a high degree of entrepreneurial drive are committed to the development of business opportunities and determined to overcome every obstacle on the path to success. Stan believed this was true of himself as well—but his actions said something else entirely. As an employee, he was accustomed to receiving a regular paycheck for a set amount of work, and he continued to have this mindset after he became a self-employed sales executive. It wasn't until his six-month transition salary had ended that he began to panic.

That is when he called me. After talking with him for a while, I decided the first step was to help Stan change his mindset from employee to business owner. Therefore, I asked him to create a written personal mission statement in which he defined exactly what he valued most and what he wanted to achieve personally and professionally. (You may want to review the sample mission statements in Chapter 2.) Stan found the process of creating a picture of how he wanted his business to look enormously helpful. He also found that it helped him focus his time and energy on the activities that best served his personal mission.

Once Stan knew what he wanted to achieve, I asked him to break this down into seven to ten Most Wanted Objectives that he could accomplish in the next twelve months. I then asked him to write down specific action steps for each one, along with a target date by which he would accomplish them. Finally, I asked Stan to review his objectives and action steps every day. If circumstances kept him from accomplishing his key tasks for the day, I asked him to note these down and then devise ways to prevent them from occurring again. Once he was close to completing a set of objectives, I asked him to create a new set to keep his momentum moving forward.

Stan now admits that when he first started this process, he didn't fully understand what was required to be successful. He didn't have any passion for what he was doing, and he felt like he was just going through the motions. Gradually he began to change. He started feeling like he was part of something larger than himself, and he discovered a new drive and energy that he'd never had before. Now each day brings Stan more opportunities to grow his practice, and he is well on the way to turning his mission Statement and most important objectives into reality.

"I now feel a deep sense of contentment with my life and where I am headed," he marvels.

Here are some additional suggestions for working with this sales success factor:

Suggestions for Working with the Entrepreneurial Drive Competency

1. Identify salespeople who demonstrate entrepreneurial drive. Choose those who take pride in being sales professionals and have a strong sense of urgency about their success. In other words, choose people who love the game! Ask them how they envision the role of a salesperson and what they think the secret of success is. Record what you learn in your *Success Factor Development Journal.*

2. In your *Success Factor Development Journal,* keep a log of situations where you feel you demonstrated entrepreneurial drive and situations where you did not. Periodically review these for patterns. Discuss them with another person and ask that person to help you assess the implications for your development.

3. Consult the literature. Read newsletters and journals related to your organization's business and the businesses of those in your marketplace. What are the trends? How can you take advantage of these trends to increase your sales? What new markets can you pursue? What greater levels of service can you provide your customers? Make notes in your Success Factor Development Journal.

4. People with entrepreneurial drive have high self-esteem, which enables them to ask for help without loss of face. Make a practice of seeking help and advice whenever you get bogged down or you encounter a seemingly insurmountable obstacle. Test your ideas with others to get help in thinking them through and to gain support.

Sales Success Factor 13: Uses Key Information Effectively

Salespeople who successfully retain large amounts of instrumental information have a thorough knowledge of their industry, their company products, and the marketplace, and they use this information strategically to achieve their goals.

Salespeople who successfully retain instrumental information:
- Get information from many sources.
- Know the right person to contact and how to get things done in their own company.
- Know the features and customer benefits of their company's products and services.
- Know what is happening with their competitors' products and services.
- Know the present needs and future trends for the marketplace their company targets.

Salespeople who LACK the skill of retaining instrumental information:
- Find it difficult to get things done in the company.
- Are surprised by shifts in the marketplace for company products.
- Do not value the importance of reading industry newsletters and journals.
- Fail to find out from customers what is happening in their company and industry.

Exercise 1: Understanding the Effective Use of Key Information Competency

To get a better understanding of how this competency works in your life, try this exercise.

Understanding Uses Key Information Effectively
Write the name of a person you know who possesses this sales success factor: ____ Describe the evidence for choosing this individual.
Write your own definition of the Uses Key Information Effectively sales success factor.

Exercise 2: Applying the Uses Key Information Effectively Competency

Now describe how you can use this competency to help you create a successful sales career.

<table>
<tr><td>How I can apply this competency in my life</td></tr>
<tr><td>

</td></tr>
</table>

Exercise 3: Practicing the Uses Key Information Effectively Competency

Now that you understand more about this competency and have a clearer picture of how it might work in your sales career, it is time to practice what you have learned by creating specific affirmations for it and spending time visualizing that it is already creating success in your career.

An example of an affirmation focused on retaining instrumental information is:

- By learning and using key information about my company, industry and marketplace, I am more successful in my career.

If you scored particularly low on certain behaviors in this category of the self-assessment test, try writing an affirmation for each one. For example:

- I collect information from many sources to use in building a successful career.
- I create a network of key people who can help me provide my clients with the best possible service.
- I understand the need for my company's products now and in the future.

Now write your own affirmations in the space below. Remember to keep them short and simple and to phrase them in the present tense as though you were describing your current reality. When you are done, sign your statement.

<table>
<tr><td>Uses Key Information Effectively Affirmations</td></tr>
<tr><td>I, _______________________________ declare that the following statements are true about me:

Signed: _______________________</td></tr>
</table>

Create A Daily Practice

Now that you have written and visualized your affirmations, the next step is to practice them regularly until they become second nature to you. Adhering to the following steps will greatly increase your ability to incorporate and apply the competency successfully in your life.

Set your intention, affirm and visualize. Take a few moments at the beginning and ending of each day to read through your affirmations, set your intention to incorporate them into your life, and visualize yourself easily and joyfully applying them in your sales career.

Write in your Daily Checklist and *Sales Success Factor Development Journal.* Make a few notes in the Morning/Evening section of your Daily Checklist (Appendix 2) and write down any additional thoughts that occur to you in your journal (Appendix 3).

Review your Sales Success Factors Development Plan. Be sure to create a Sales Success Factors Development Plan (Appendix 4) to help you develop this competency. Then review it daily to make sure you are on track.

Reassess, Reward, Revise, And Repeat

After practicing your affirmations for a few weeks, reassess how you are doing on the core behaviors of this competency. If you feel that you now use all aspects of the core behaviors effectively, reward yourself. If you need more work, write a new affirmation to target the core behaviors that are still weak. Then begin the cycle again.

Case Study: Commit To Lifelong Learning

When Richard entered the financial services business as a transplant from another industry, he accepted the fact that his learning curve would be steep. Therefore, he willingly put in the time and sweat equity it took to learn the fundamentals. He survived his early years in the business, but after seven years realized he was stagnating and that the quality of his current prospects was of the same caliber as when he had first started out. In effect, he had had seven one-year experiences instead of seven years of experience.

I explained to Richard that today more than ever, the pace of change is speeding up. I agreed that it was impossible for him to keep up with everything; however, I also said that it was imperative for him to stay current *in his own profession and specialty.* I remarked that he had become a generalist who had never taken the time and effort necessary to grow professionally. In today's competitive marketplace, with increasingly savvy consumers, it is critical, I said, to become a *lifelong* learner.

To get started, I suggested that he select one or two aspects of his practice that he especially liked. He told me that he had a personal interest in charitable giving, so he decided to begin a program of study that would lead to special designations in this field. Richard then began prospecting for people who were interested in leaving a legacy to their favorite organization or cause. He also went back to his existing clients and told them that he had developed expertise in this new area of specialization. Some wanted to learn more about this for themselves, and others referred him to people they knew who could benefit from his specialization.

After just one year, Richard has completely transformed his practice. Today he is excited again about where his career is heading, he's attracting much higher quality prospects, and he's proud about the value he is offering.

The moral of this story is that training and education are never onetime events. Make time for them regularly in your practice, and you will be amply rewarded for your efforts.

Here are some additional suggestions for working with this sales success factor:

Suggestions for Working with Effective Use of Key Information Competency

1. Identify salespeople in your organization who are successful at building the value of customer relationships and ask them how they identify "high potential" customers and develop mutually beneficial relationships with them. In your Success Factor Development Journal, write down how you will apply this information to increase the value of these relationships.
2. Make a point to seek out and introduce yourself to key home office people at company meetings.
3. Select areas of expertise you would like to develop that involve departments within your organization. Find experts in these areas who will let you observe them for a while. Watch what they do and ask them questions about their job. Afterwards, jot down ideas in your Success Factor Development Journal about how you can work more effectively with them and their departments. As questions arise, jot them down and get the answers from your contacts.
4. You can also use your observation lists to develop a checklist of the people to see to get things done in your company and what questions to ask them.
5. Examine how much time you spend keeping up with trends in your industry and marketplace. Are you consistently learning about your company's products and the latest applications relevant to your clients so you can be effective in generating new business? Develop some goals and jot them down in your Success Factor Development Journal to keep you on track for getting the information that is key to your success.
6. Develop a plan to become knowledgeable about a competitor's products in your area of expertise. Read about these products and talk to others who have used them.
7. Ask your manager to share insights about other groups in the company with whom you will be working. Where does a particular group fit into the overall organization? Could company politics impact your success in working with that group?

Sales Success Factor 14: Increases Customer Value

Salespeople who excel at increasing customer value are able to take advantage of high potential customer relationships and create added value—both for their customers and for their own businesses.

Salespeople who excel at increasing customer value:
- Leverage their sales to gain additional business.
- Work to assure that good customers continue to do business with them.
- Maintain contact with their clients; as a result, they know when there are new opportunities to pursue or problems to solve.
- Proactively and regularly bring to their customers' attention the services and products that are available to meet their needs.
- Understand their customers, which enables them to impact their customers' organizations dramatically.

Salespeople who LACK skill in increasing customer value:
- Forget the customer once the sale is made.
- Find that their customers start doing business with their company's competitors.
- Never make a follow-up sale to a client.
- Are constantly chasing new prospects and complain that their old customers are not loyal to them.

Exercise 1: Understanding the Increases Customer Value Competency

To get a better understanding of how this competency works in your life, try this exercise.

Understanding Increases Customer Value
Write the name of a person you know who possesses this sales success factor: ___________________________________ Describe the evidence for choosing this individual.
Write your own definition of the Increases Customer Value sales success factor.

Exercise 2: Applying the Increases Customer Value Competency

Now describe how you can use this competency to help you create a successful sales career.

How I can apply this competency in my life

Exercise 3: Practicing the Increases Customer Value Competency

Now that you understand more about this competency and have a clearer picture of how it might work in your sales career, it is time to practice what you have learned by creating specific affirmations for it and spending time visualizing that it is already creating success in your career.

An example of an affirmation focused on increases customer value is:
- Because I recognize that loyal customers are one of my organization's greatest assets, I am wired to my most valuable customers, stay in touch with their needs for our products, and provide them with optimal service.

If you scored particularly low on certain behaviors in this category of the self-assessment test, try writing an affirmation for each one. For example:
- I stay in touch and make an effort to see that my good customers continue to do business with my organization.
- I make a continual effort to understand how my customers' organizations accomplish their business goals and to let them know how my products and services can help them do so.
- I make sure that my first sale to a client leads to additional sales.

Now write your own affirmations in the space below. Remember to keep them short and simple and to phrase them in the present tense as though you were describing your current reality. When you are done, sign your statement.

Increases Customer Value Affirmations

I, _________________________________ declare that the following statements are true about me:

Signed: _______________________________

Create A Daily Practice

Now that you have written and visualized your affirmations, the next step is to practice them regularly until they become second nature to you. Adhering to the following steps will greatly increase your ability to incorporate and apply the competency successfully in your life.

> **Set your intention, affirm and visualize.** Take a few moments at the beginning and ending of each day to read through your affirmations, set your intention to incorporate them into your life, and visualize yourself easily and joyfully applying them in your sales career.

Write in your Daily Checklist and *Sales Success Factor Development Journal.* Make a few notes in the Morning/Evening section of your Daily Checklist (Appendix 2) and write down any additional thoughts that occur to you in your journal (Appendix 3).

Review your Sales Success Factors Development Plan. Be sure to create a Sales Success Factors Development Plan (Appendix 4) to help you develop this competency. Then review it daily to make sure you are on track.

Reassess, Reward, Revise, And Repeat

After practicing your affirmations for a few weeks, reassess how you are doing on the core behaviors of this competency. If you feel that you now use all aspects of the core behaviors effectively, reward yourself. If you need more work, write a new affirmation to target the core behaviors that are still weak. Then begin the cycle again.

Case Study: Maintaining Contact With Your Clients

 Derrick got off to a fast start in his insurance practice and soon had above average selling activity. He successfully leveraged his networking connections to meet new people and make sales and was considered an above average salesman in his office. After five years, he had developed a decent clientele, both in quantity and quality.

Over time, however, his sales activity gradually began to slow down. Whenever times were tough, he brought out the list of clients he hadn't spoken to recently and called them for an appointment. He was shocked when some of their reactions were less than enthusiastic. In fact, some had actually purchased additional products or services from other financial professionals!

After talking with Derrick for a while, I realized that he had become a bit lazy and lost sight of how providing consistent customer value could catapult his practice to the next level. We reviewed what he had promised each of his clients after his first sale to them: to keep in touch with them regularly and to make sure that their insurance and financial objectives were always up-to-date. Clearly, he had failed to do this.

To remedy the situation, I suggested that Derrick put a system in place that would remind him to connect with each of his prospects and clients at least twice a year. In addition, I suggested that he keep his customers in mind every time he attended a training session, conference, or seminar on a product or service. I suggested that he think about and write down the names of prospects and clients who might benefit from what he was learning, then call them up and ask for the opportunity to share it with them.

Once Derrick got into the habit of applying such ideas to his practice, good things began to occur. Because he met with his clients regularly, they felt valued, became loyal to him, and purchased more products. They were also less likely to give their business to the competition. Derrick also felt good about asking for the names of others who could benefit from this information, and his clients readily responded with referrals.

Here are some additional suggestions for working with this sales success factor:

Suggestions for Working with the Increases Customer Value Competency

1. Identify sales people in your organization who are particularly good at increasing customer value. Interview them to find out what they do to build the value of their customer portfolio. In your Success Factor Development Journal, make some notes on what you learn in the interviews and outline some action steps that you will follow to apply these ideas to your own sales efforts.
2. For many sales people, the difficulty of achieving profitable career growth is not a matter of running too slowly, but of chasing the wrong customers—those who are unprofitable to serve because they drain resources and effort for minimal results. So be selective and do your due diligence.
3. Instead of running after customers, run with them by understanding where they want to go and how you can help them get there.
4. Include your customers when you are developing a solution for a business problem they have.
5. Schedule time to keep up with new developments in your industry and new customer needs. Read the marketing materials from your own company as well as those of your competitors. How can you apply what you read to strengthening relationships with your high quality customers? Record your thoughts in your Success Factor Development Journal.
6. Talk to each of your high quality clients and ask them how you can serve them better.
7. Keep files on your clients and systematically review them with an eye to discovering present and future needs. Devise a system to keep in touch with them on a consistent basis. Also prepare an effective strategy to present your solutions to them.
8. Create a procedure to track customer issues as they arise. Be sure to follow up to ensure that you address these issues promptly and effectively.
9. Think about what you have done in the past year to showcase your company to your customers. Did they feel a sense of excitement about the emerging capabilities of your organization? Plan some educational activities for your key account customers.

Sales Success Factor 15: Builds a Team

Salespeople who excel at building teams develop strong formal and informal relationships that help them achieve their sales career mission.

Salespeople who excel at building teams:
- Build deep, long-term relationships that can be leveraged for later work.
- Readily share directions and suggestions to help others maximize their potential and recognize their options.
- Provide task focus and direction and ensure that staff members understand performance standards.
- Create an environment where people can work together to meet organizational goals and feel they are part of a team.
- Promote cooperation and collaboration between individuals and groups.

Salespeople who LACK the skill of building teams:
- Consider the effort to develop staff members a waste of time.
- Fail to give people specific feedback about how their actions help or hinder team effort.
- Avoid confrontation and have a hard time resolving conflicts with other team members.
- Prefer working alone and dislike coordinating with others.

Exercise 1: Understanding the Builds a Team Competency

To get a better understanding of how this competency works in your life, try this exercise.

Understanding Builds a Team
Write the name of a person you know who possesses this sales success factor: ____ Describe the evidence for choosing this individual.
Write your own definition of the Builds a Team sales success factor.

Exercise 2: Applying the Builds a Team Competency

Now describe how you can use this competency to help you create a successful sales career.

How I can apply this competency in my life

Exercise 3: Practicing the Builds a Team Competency

Now that you understand more about this competency and have a clearer picture of how it might work in your sales career, it is time to practice what you have learned by creating specific affirmations for it and spending time visualizing that it is already creating success in your career.

An example of an affirmation focused on building a team is:
- I constantly work to strengthen formal and informal relationships with people on whom I can call to form a team that will support my goals and mission.

If you scored particularly low on certain behaviors in this category of the self-assessment test, try writing an affirmation for each one. For example:
- I am always ready to share directions and suggestions to help the people I work with maximize their potential and recognize their options.
- I make sure that staff members understand their roles and the standards they are expected to meet.
- I am good at creating a work environment where people can work together to meet organizational goals.

Now write your own affirmations in the space below. Remember to keep them short and simple and to phrase them in the present tense as though you were describing your current reality. When you are done, sign your statement.

Builds a Team Affirmations

I, ________________________________ declare that the following statements are true about me:

Signed: ________________________________

Create A Daily Practice

Now that you have written and visualized your affirmations, the next step is to practice them regularly until they become second nature to you. Adhering to the following steps will greatly increase your ability to incorporate and apply the competency successfully in your life.

Set your intention, affirm and visualize. Take a few moments at the beginning and ending of each day to read through your affirmations, set your intention to incorporate them into your life, and visualize yourself easily and joyfully applying them in your sales career.

Write in your Daily Checklist and *Sales Success Factor Development Journal.* Make a few notes in the Morning/Evening section of your Daily Checklist (Appendix 2) and write down any additional thoughts that occur to you in your journal (Appendix 3).

Review your Sales Success Factors Development Plan. Be sure to create a Sales Success Factors Development Plan (Appendix 4) to help you develop this competency. Then review it daily to make sure you are on track.

Reassess, Reward, Revise, And Repeat

After practicing your affirmations for a few weeks, reassess how you are doing on the core behaviors of this competency. If you feel that you now use all aspects of the core behaviors effectively, reward yourself. If you need more work, write a new affirmation to target the core behaviors that are still weak. Then begin the cycle again.

Case Study: Developing successful team leadership skills

Many types of teams exist in the workplace. Some are formal, others are informal. Some are created by your own choosing, while others are predetermined. Most salespeople start their sales career as an individual contributor who is solely responsible for doing what is necessary to succeed.

Once they have mastered the basics and their practices grow, however, they often find they don't have enough hours in the day to accomplish all that needs to be done. In addition, they discover they are spending most of their time on the least productive, least profitable activities.

Eventually, they come to the conclusion that they need to hire some employees. But the transition to employer can be challenging. The fact that successful salespeople are accustomed to going it alone as individual contributors is the same reason why so many have such a difficult time building a successful team.

George's Story

George knew he had come to the point that he had to multiply himself if he was to grow his practice, so he hired a part-time assistant. After just two months, he concluded that all he had accomplished was to increase his overhead, so he let the assistant go. The work continued to pile up, however, so a few months later he tried again. After just one month, George was beside himself. He was working harder and putting in longer hours than ever before, but he was accomplishing less.

This is when he contacted me. After talking with him for a while, I realized that George subscribed to the "shooting from the hip" style of management. His communications to his assistant were unclear and disorganized, and he often gave her conflicting assignments. He also maintained that it was easier for him to do a task himself than to take the time to train her to do it properly. No wonder George was unhappy with this arrangement!

To help him turn the situation around, I asked him to create a written job description for his assistant that began with a clear summary of what the position entailed. Then I suggested that he create a specific, detailed list of job tasks and responsibilities, along with a description of how each task was to be accomplished. As he worked through this process, George's priorities became crystal clear; for the first time, he understood what doing a good job for him actually looked like.

George's next step was to go over the job description with his assistant. Although he was apprehensive at first, the meeting went extremely well. "My assistant was really pleased that I had taken the time to write down my expectations of her," he said. "She said she had been frustrated, too, because she did not know if she was doing a good job for me or not. Now we both have a fair way to judge her performance."

This experience helped George realize that working effectively with an assistant required better preparation and organization on his part first. This included taking the time to figure out the tools and resources she needed to be successful. He also came to the realization that investing the time it took to train her was a win-win situation because it would make her more efficient and give him more time in front of his prospects.

Grace's Story

Grace had a different problem. She and a partner had owned a business together for many years. One of his responsibilities was to oversee the staff, so Grace paid little attention to what he did in this area or how he did it. Unfortunately, the partner became seriously ill and decided to retire early, so Grace bought out his half of the partnership.

For the next seven months, she ran the business solo. She gradually began to notice, however, that tension was growing in the office between staff members. Work was not getting done on time, mistakes began to rise, and she always seemed to find herself stepping in to settle arguments between employees.

Mystified by what was happening, she turned to me for help. I observed that she, like George, had always been a solo practitioner. Grace admitted that one of the main reasons she had taken on a partner in the first place was to help her in the areas in which she was deficient. Clearly, building a team was one of them.

I explained to her that in my experience, 85% of office problems are due to process and just 15% to people. I asked her to read *The Team Handbook, How to Use Teams to Improve Quality* by Peter Scholtes, which presents the Ten Ingredients for a Successful Team:

1. Clarity in Team Goals
2. Clearly Defined Roles
3. Clear Communication
4. Beneficial Team Behaviors
5. An Improvement Plan
6. Well Defined Decision Procedures
7. Balanced Participation
8. Established Ground Rules
9. Awareness of the Group Process
10. Use of the Scientific Approach

To improve the process issue in Grace's practice, I asked her to work on the first four ingredients for a successful team listed above. Her first assignment was to meet with her staff to discuss, agree on, and write down what each of these ingredients meant to them. The clarity that they gained from this process had an immediately positive effect, and they began working with each other much more effectively and harmoniously.

To improve Grace's leadership skills, I asked her to read the following article, which I wrote for the July 2007 edition of *Champions' E-zine:*

We are indeed fortunate to be in a profession that allows us to "help others along the way." Whether you are a producer or a manager, you can have a positive impact upon those you serve. To do so takes leadership.

In a 1965 lecture titled "A Business and Its Beliefs—The Ideas that Helped Build IBM," Thomas J. Watson, Jr. said:

"Belief and philosophy constitute a transcendent factor which outweighs technology, economic resources, or anything else in achieving success. This then is my thesis. I firmly believe that any organization, in order to survive and achieve success, must have a sound set of beliefs on which it premises all its policies and actions...In other words, the basic philosophy, spirit, and drive of an organization have far more to do with its relative achievements than do technological or economic resources, organizational structure, innovation, and timing. All these things weigh heavily in success. But they are, I think, transcended by how strongly the people in the organization believe in its basic precepts and how faithfully they carry them out."

What is your definition of leadership? Mine is:
- Building and developing people
- Getting things done through people
- Understanding the power of your own beliefs and how those beliefs influence your own and others' productivity

I believe that everyone is looking for someone to ask them to become all that they are capable of becoming. This is one of the greatest gifts you can give to another person.

If you are looking to increase your leadership skills, consider the following leadership core values. View the following statements as a mini self-assessment. Rate yourself on a scale of 1-10 where a "1" means that you seldom or never think or act in the way described and a "10" means that you most often or always think or act this way.

- **I believe that people have unlimited positive potential**. Seeing more in people than they see in themselves is often the key factor that sparks that extra inner drive that propels people to achieve more than they ever thought was possible.
- **I believe that people are basically good.** I have found that most people are doing the very best that they can on any given day. View them in a positive light.
- **I believe that people give back to us the same attitudes and responses we give them.** This is the law of psychological reciprocity. Most people start liking us about the same time they feel that we like and respect them.
- **I believe that people deeply desire having meaning and significance in their lives.** Most people want to make a difference in their personal and/or business life; they want to be a part of something bigger than themselves. Are you tapping into this most basic human instinct?
- **I believe that people respond positively to positive leadership**. Most people I speak to assume that they have a positive influence on others. This is not always the case. Sometimes our actions get out of alignment with our words.
- **I believe that people feel good about themselves when they take responsibility and keep their commitments.** This can sometimes test your leadership skills because it is hard to do. It raises the bar of responsibility and places that responsibility on others. Our job is to provide the support, training, encouragement and inspiration. We can't do it for them. If we do, it only serves to diminish confidence and self-respect.

Self First

It all begins with you. Before challenging others, challenge yourself. Are you the best that you can be? Do you bring out the best in others? Do you lead by example? You will achieve what you believe and feel passionate about.

Would you like to improve your leadership skills? Consider these additional suggestions:
- Know who you are and where you're going.
- Know your vision and mission statement.
- Leverage your strengths.
- Be positive and become a positive influence.
- See the best in others.
- Be a lifelong learner and always seek to grow personally and professionally.
- Admit mistakes and learn from them.
- Be a great listener. Seek first to understand others and then to be understood by others.
- Always act in harmony with your values.

After she had read this article, I asked Grace to score herself on each of the key points. Over the months that followed, she worked hard to understand the leadership behaviors and attitudes expressed in each point and to apply them with her team. This had several major benefits. First, her team made great improvements in quality, performance and overall job satisfaction. Second, she made great personal strides as her knowledge of leadership and human relations grew. Finally—because of the improvements both she and her staff were making—her clients became happier, and her practice expanded.

Here are some additional suggestions for working with this sales success factor:

Suggestions for Working with the Builds a Team Competency

1. Look around your organization and identify salespeople in positions similar to yours who are particularly effective in building successful teams with others. Interview them to find out how they do it. In your Success Factor Development Journal, make some notes about what you learn from them. Then prepare some action steps for your own sales career. Here are some questions to ask:
   - What have you done to encourage cooperation and discourage a "this-is-not-my-job" attitude among the people who support your sales efforts?
   - What have you done to help the people who support your sales effort develop their on-the-job effectiveness?
   - What have you done to give directions and set standards for the people who support you?
2. Do the people who support your sales efforts understand your values, philosophy and general expectations? If not, share these with them.
3. Whenever you have a goal or deadline that involves the cooperation of others, make a conscious effort to build a good team. Identify the people who are on the team and determine their working styles. Talk to them or to others who have worked with them. Also decide how to adjust your own style to build the most effective team.

Suggestions for Working with the Builds a Team Competency, continued

4. Find enjoyable and creative ways to celebrate with the people who help you achieve a victory. Be sure to praise individuals for their good work.
5. Keep your eyes open for times when people who work with or for you go out of their way to be helpful to each other or to people in other parts of the company. Find a way to acknowledge and reinforce their positive teamwork and cooperation.
6. Should illness or tragedy strike any of the people with whom you work, look for ways to keep in touch with them so they know they are not forgotten.

Chapter 9 # Conclusion

Congratulations! You have now taken the steps necessary to experience and accelerate your journey to success. You have made a deliberate decision to choose personal growth and continual professional development over complacency and the status quo. Acknowledge yourself for what you have accomplished. You should feel proud!

Choosing the path of growth and improvement isn't easy. It requires introspection and courage, as well as discipline and a deep commitment to changing behavior and habits. I hope this book has helped you discover your strengths as well as the areas that need improvement. I also hope it has given you the tools, ideas, and motivation you need to achieve your personal and business goals—today and into the future.

As I explained in the Introduction, there are six prerequisites for success in a sales career. These prerequisites are not something you do once, check off a list, and forget. Instead, they describe a cycle you must practice again and again. The great thing about this is that each time you do, you will discover more about yourself, gain new insights and inspiration, and move to higher and higher levels of achievement. In other words, the six prerequisites represent the map to your journey through life, not just to a single destination.

In review, the six prerequisites are:

An unwavering commitment to a sales career mission that is in line with your personal values. It is my hope that you now have an even stronger personal sales career mission because it is aligned with your values. Success in sales requires much more than application of mechanical techniques. It demands a deep inner belief that you are part of something bigger than yourself and that you are contributing something of great value.

A vision that provides a detailed mental picture of the future you want to create for your sales career as you pursue your mission. Walt Disney is often quoted as saying, "If you can dream it, you can do it." I agree with him. I would also add that you have to visualize it, verbalize it, and feel the emotions that come from the imagined success of having already attained it. Just as world-class athletes visualize the successful accomplishment of their goals, so must you.

Clearly-defined goals in which you specify what you need to achieve to make your vision a reality. Many salespeople I work with resist the idea of writing down their goals, let alone making them clear and specific. Perhaps this has to do more with accountability or fear of failure than it does with overall resistance to the idea or an inability to plan. If this is true for you, remember the story I told in Chapter 6 (Case Study for the Results Orientation) about the three percent of the 1956 graduates of Yale University who experienced remarkably more success than their classmates simply because they wrote down their goals throughout their lives.

Mastery of the sales success factors, or the behaviors, motives, attitudes, traits, and self-concepts that contribute to superior sales performance. Mastery comes with practice, dedication to life-long learning, and a drive for continuous improvement. Just being good enough or possessing average skills won't cut it in today's super-competitive, ever-changing marketplace. The sales profession demands excellence. Settle for nothing less.

Action plans that provide road maps. Vision and mission statements are the "what," while action plans are the "how." You can use these maps to access people and resources, as well as to practice the sales success factors that will enable you to achieve your goals. Remember that your action plans don't need to be long or elaborate—simple bullet points will do. Whatever form they take, be sure that they include actionable, measurable steps, each of which has a target deadline date. If you miss your deadline, don't beat yourself up for it or let it derail you. Simply ask yourself why you missed it and listen for the answer. It also helps to spend some time re-visualizing how wonderful you will feel once you have achieved the goal(s) attached to your action plan. Then set a new, more realistic target date and begin again.

A way to maintain progress on the journey until your vision of success becomes reality. This book has given you numerous tools, techniques and exercises to help you keep your goals foremost in your mind and to track your progress. Whether you use the ones I have suggested or create your own, it's imperative that you find a way to keep score. Anything that gets measured can be improved. A story I hear far too often from new clients is that they set goals at the beginning of each year and then fail to look at them again until the end of year. Tracking your progress along the way is critical to reaching your destination with a minimum of wrong turns and with maximum efficiency and effectiveness.

Working with an Accountability Partner

Working with an accountability partner is a particularly powerful way to maintain your progress on the journey. Your partner might be a colleague, spouse, friend, or coach. Make sure you choose someone whom you trust and respect and who wants the best for you. The extra octane this additional measure of accountability gives you will greatly speed up your journey to success.

A Final Word

Now that you have completed the roadmap laid out in this book, you have discovered many new things about yourself. You have also developed new levels of awareness and practical skills that will serve you well. Remember that the journey you are embarking on is a never-ending process. This is why it is well to become a student of life and of your business. Remember that while change is inevitable, growth is optional. It is all up to you. Good luck on your journey to success!

Contact Bob Arzt, CLU, ChFC, LLIF

Insurance Coach U™
10216 Sweetwood Ave.
Rockville, MD 20850
Phone: 301-610-5624
Fax: 301-610-5625
bob@insurancecoachu.com
www.insurancecoachu.com

Do you have a success story of how you have used *What Every Great Salesperson Knows?*

If so, I'd love to hear from you. (I might also use your story in a future edition of this book.) Please send your success stories to me via e-mail or snail mail.

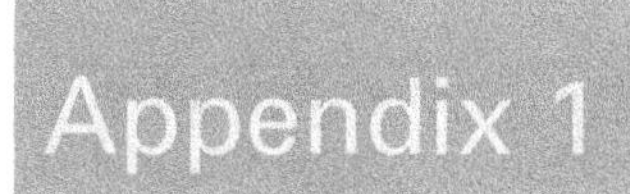
Ideal Work Week Exercise

The Ideal Work Week exercise helps your track your activities so you understand where your time is actually going.

To create it, begin by reviewing your appointment calendar for the last 30 to 60 days and writing down how you spent your time each day. One way to reconstruct your schedule is to analyze your office activities, such as the time you spent on paperwork or case preparation. Another way is to track your time for the next 30 days and then use this information to construct your ideal work week.

The more accurately and precisely you track your activities (such as hour by hour), the better you will understand where your time goes, what your priorities are, and how to be more effective and efficient with your time.

Once you have some data to work with, combine similar tasks into categories. For example, you could combine activities like reviewing applications and filling out tracking reports into one category named "administration."

Then calculate the amount of time you invest in each category and convert it to the average amount of time you spend each week in each category. For example:

Current Work Week	
Activity	Time
Laser Planning*	0.5
Administration	12.0
Training / Professional Development	1.0
Appointments	10.0
Appointments	6.0
Telephoning	2.0
Case Preparation	4.5
Fail Safe/Catch Up	1.0
Health	2.0
Misc.	21.0
Total	60.0

*Note: Laser Planning means setting aside 10 to 20 minutes each day to review your day's activities and to schedule appropriate time during the week to accomplish what needs to get done.

Convert the average number of hours you invest each week into the percentage it represents of your work week. Then graph your results in a pie chart. To do so, either use a spreadsheet application like Excel or simply draw a pie chart by hand.

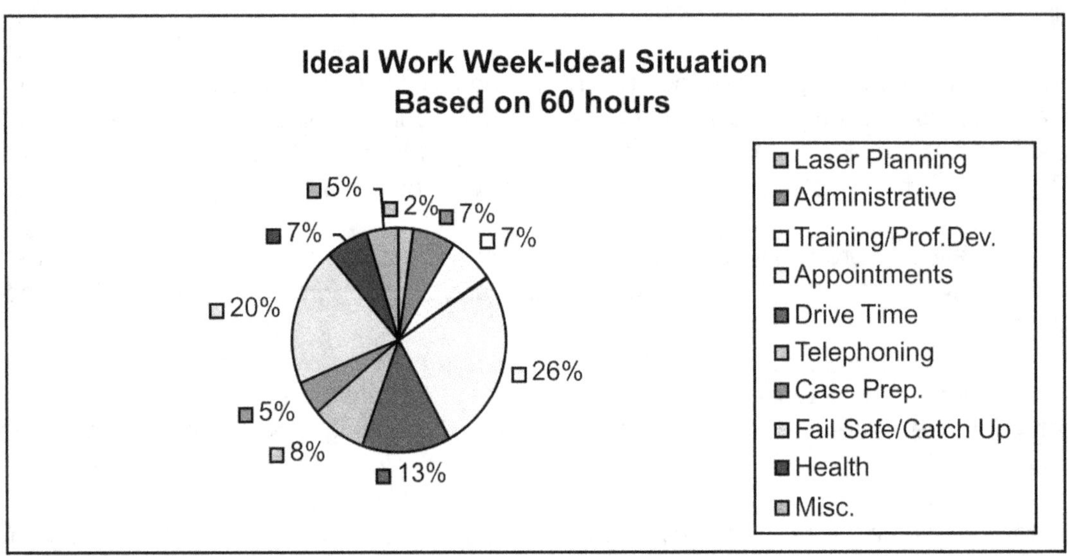

Now create an Ideal Work Week Schedule using the same categories as above. To decide what's ideal for you, you will need to determine the amount of sales activity that is required to achieve your production goals. (For a more detailed explanation of how to set and achieve your goals, refer to the Results Orientation Sales Factor in Chapter 6.)

Ideal Work Week Schedule	
Activity	Time
Laser Planning*	1.25
Administration	4.0
Training / Professional Development	4.0
Appointments	16.0
Appointments	8.0
Telephoning	5.0
Case Preparation	3.0
Fail Safe/Catch Up	12.0
Health	4.0
Misc.	2.75
Total	60.0

The next step is to turn your ideal work week into a graph:

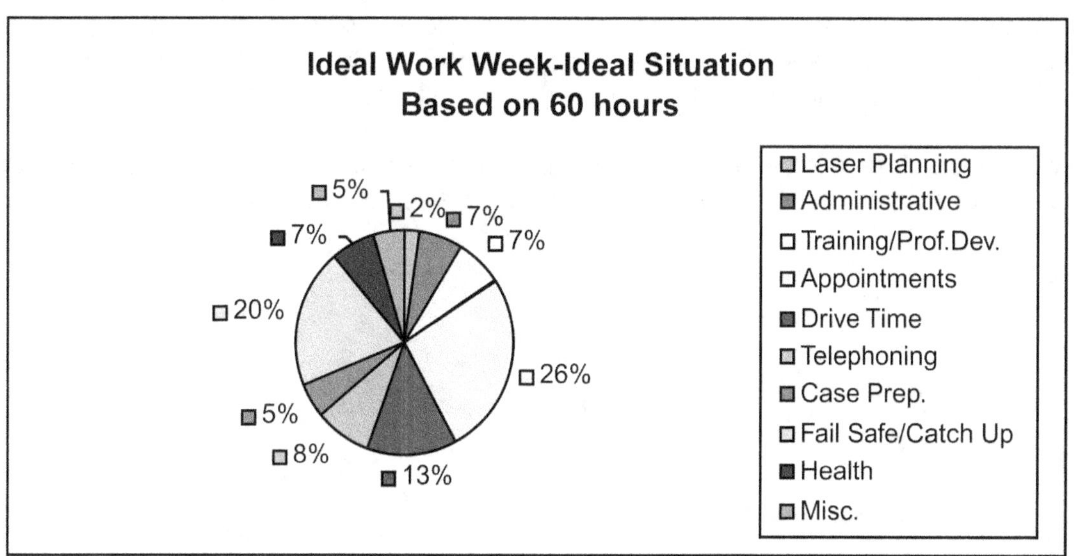

Then compare your Current Work Week allocation of time to your Ideal Work Week allocation of time. This will help you determine which categories of time you need to devote more attention to. Then plot your Ideal Work Week on an actual calendar. For example:

Sample Ideal Work Week (Copyright © 2009 Polaris One)

	Monday	Tuesday	Wednesday	Thursday	Friday	Saturday
7:00-7:15am	Laser Planning	Laser Planning	Laser Planning	Laser Planning	Laser Planning	Optional Fail Safe Time
8:00 am	Administration	Telephone	Appointment 8-9	Telephone	Administration	Catch Up
9:00 am			Appointment 9:30-10:30			Administration
10:00 am	Training	Appointment 10:30-11:30		Appointment 10:30-11:30	Professional Development	Telephone
11:00 am	Meeting		Appointment 11-12			Planning Other
12:00 pm	Appointment 12-1	Appointment 12-1	Appointment 12:30-1:30	Appointment 12-1	Fail Safe Time	
1:00 pm		Appointment 1:30-2:30		Appointment 1:30-2:30	Catch Up	
2:00 pm	Appointment 1:30-2:30		Appointment 2-3		Administration	
3:00 pm		Appointment 3-4	Administration	Appointment 3-4	Personal	
4:00 pm	Appointment 4-5	Telephone			Get Ahead	
5:00 pm	Case Prep.	Gym	Case Prep.	Gym	Other	
6:00 pm						
7:00 pm	Open	Open	Open	Open	Open	

Time Summary

Laser Planning	1.25 hrs.	Telephoning:	5.00 hrs.
Administration	4.00 hrs.	Case Prep:	3.00 hrs.
Training/Professional Development	4.00 hrs.	Fail Safe/Catch up:	12.00 hrs.
Appointments	16.00 hrs.	Health:	4.00 hrs.

Finally, transfer your Ideal Work Week to your actual appointment calendar.

Commit yourself to closely following your Ideal Work Week schedule, treating it the same as you would an actual appointment with a client or prospect. For example, if during Laser Planning on Monday morning you determine that you need 45 minutes to prepare the Tom Smith case, then write in "Tom Smith" in the specific Case Preparation time block where you need to complete the work.

Finally, reward yourself for a job well done! Maintaining the discipline to adhere to your Ideal Work Week schedule will not only increase your bottom line, but it will also add more constructive hours to your day.

Appendix 2   The Daily Checklist

Morning	Date/ Time:
My mission:	
Considering my mission, what are my specific goals for today?	
What steps do I need to take to accomplish these goals?	
What skills/people/assistance do I need to carry this out?	

Evening	Date/ Time:
How well did I do at implementing my specific goals for the day? What worked? What didn't?	
How can I improve tomorrow? What do I need to do next?	

Appendix 3 — The Sales Success Factor Development Journal

As stated in Chapter 2, writing helps us acquire new knowledge and synthesize it so it becomes part of us. It helps us discover what we really think and feel about a subject, and it helps us come up with insights that would otherwise have remained unconscious if we had not written them down.

The act of writing down our dreams, ideas, insights, hunches, goals, action steps, questions and congratulations for our successes is an invaluable tool that soon becomes a welcome daily ritual and record of how far we have come. (Be sure to date each entry.)

To get started, print enough copies of the following form for the coming week. Punch three holes on the left margin and place the copies in a 3-ring binder.

To start the creative juices flowing, think about one or more of the following topics and simply write down what you see, feel, think or hear.
- Your short and long range goals
- Your personal vision and/or mission statement
- Tasks you need to undertake to achieve specific goals
- Congratulations for your accomplishments
- Ideas, hunches, insights
- Questions you want answered

Good luck on your journey to success!

Sales Success Factors Development Journal

Date _______________________

Sales Success Factors Development Journal

Date _______________________

The Sales Success Factors Development Plan

Following are examples of how to use the Sales Success Factors Development Plan. On the next page, you will find blank forms that you can copy and use for yourself. (Be sure to specify a date on your goal statement by which you will have accomplished your objective.)

Sales Success Factor: Managing Yourself: Shows Self-Discipline

Goal Statement: By June 1st I will create and follow an Ideal Work Week schedule

Action Item	Create an Ideal Work Week Schedule
Potential Obstacles	None—just set aside time to create it
Sources of Help	Review my Ideal Work Week with my manager
Measurements & Time Frames	Complete by May 1st

Sales Success Factor: Managing Yourself: Shows Self-Discipline

Goal Statement: By June 1st I will create and follow an Ideal Work Week schedule

Action Item	Create an Ideal Work Week Schedule
Potential Obstacles	None—just set aside time to create it
Sources of Help	Review my Ideal Work Week with my manager
Measurements & Time Frames	Complete by May 1st

Sales Success Factor: ____

Goal Statement: ____

Action Item	
Potential Obstacles	
Sources of Help	
Measurements & Time Frames	

Sales Success Factor: ____

Goal Statement: ____

Action Item	
Potential Obstacles	
Sources of Help	
Measurements & Time Frames	

Sales Success Factor: ____

Goal Statement: ____

Action Item	
Potential Obstacles	
Sources of Help	
Measurements & Time Frames	

Helping Insurance Professionals Navigate the Road to Success

InsuranceCoachU© is dedicated to the insurance industry. Whether you are new to the industry, a seasoned insurance professional, producer or manager, InsuranceCoachU© has resources and answers that will dramatically impact you and your business.

Champions' E-Zine - Inspiration Delivered!

Bob Arzt, creator of **Champions' Success Groups©**, is a passionate collector of quotes, thoughts, and ideas that can have a positive and compelling influence on your life. Each month he shares these thought-provoking ideas in his monthly newsletter called *Champions E-zine. Champions* celebrates the fact that when positive thoughts and ideas are put into action, they lead to a positive, productive, fulfilling, and satisfying life.

Free Teleclasses

InsuranceCoachU periodically conducts free 45-60 minute teleclasses that cover a specific topic of interest. Classes are conducted using a blended learning approach of lecture and group participation.

Champions' Success Groups© For Insurance Sales and Management Professionals- Course Descriptions

Champions' Success Groups© are Mastermind Groups that will inspire you to achieve at a higher level. Get encouragement, be coached by an insurance expert, listen to what has worked for others and learn how to follow a game plan with the support and advice of peers. Whether you are interested in increasing sales, improving insurance agency and unit operations, or accelerating the achievement of your goals, Champions' Success Groups© are for you. Our proven formula has worked for others, and it can work for you as well!

Courses and Programs

InsuranceCoachU can help your organization create custom training and development programs that get long-term results. We believe that for training to be effective, organizations must develop the systems and secure the support at all levels that are necessary to ensure that you successfully implement your programs, increase your skills and obtain results.

Individual Coaching

Champions have a coach and teammates. Who is helping you succeed as an insurance professional? In my many years in the insurance industry, I have managed, recruited and trained producers and managers; I have also coached and counseled many agents and managers to successful careers. As a result, I know how to grow an insurance practice, and I am familiar with the problems and issues you face. This means I can give you more than just general motivational advice. Be coached by an expert and get real results.